I0528531

www.ingramcontent.com/pod-product-compliance
Lightning Source LLC
Chambersburg PA
CBHW051332120626
46547CB00016B/2507

* 9 7 8 1 9 5 7 1 0 9 4 3 5 *

דניאל

THE
ISRAEL
BIBLE

DANIEL

EDITED BY

Rabbi Tuly Weisz

ISRAEL
365

The Israel Bible: Daniel

First Edition, 2021

The Israel Bible was produced by Israel365 in cooperation with Teach for
Israel and is used with permission from Teach for Israel. All rights reserved.
The English translation was adapted by Israel365 from the JPS Tanakh.
Copyright © 1985 by the Jewish Publication Society. All rights reserved.

Cover image used under license from Shutterstock.com

ISBN 978-1-957109-43-5

A CIP catalogue record for this title is available from the British Library

The Israel Bible: Daniel is a holy book that contains the
name of God and should be treated with respect.

Table of Contents

Introduction

The Hebrew Bible is commonly known as the *Tanakh* which stands for *Torah* (the Five Books of Moses), *Neviim* (the Prophets) and *Ketuvim* (the Writings). The *Tanakh* consists of 24 books that are considered by Jews to be the word of God. While these books have been referred to as the "Old Testament," many Jews reject this label since it implies the replacement of the Hebrew Bible with something newer and prefer the more authentic Jewish name.

The *Tanakh* is not only the most important book known to man, it is God's word that is perfect and absolute. It is therefore a daunting undertaking to publish an edition of the *Tanakh*, and the responsibilities are awesome. There is no room for error or carelessness in dealing with the eternal word of God. Further, upon embarking on such a serious initiative, we ask ourselves if our efforts are gratuitous. Considering the many editions of the Bible in print, is there truly a need for yet another one?

While there are numerous Bibles in circulation today, its most central aspect – the Land of Israel – has often been overlooked. References to Israel appear on nearly every page, and the city of Jerusalem is specifically referred to hundreds of times throughout the Bible. The essential link between Israel and *Torah* is emphasized repeatedly in verses such as, "For instruction (*Torah*) shall come forth from *Tzion*, the word of *Hashem* from *Yerushalayim*" (Micah 4:2).

The miraculous return of the People of Israel to the Land of Israel in our own generation provides the perfect moment for a new volume to fill this void in biblical literature. *The Israel Bible* includes many special features elucidating God's focus on Israel throughout *Tanakh* and there are many additional, multimedia features available on our website **www.theisraelbible.com**.

Ordering and Presentation – In presenting *The Israel Bible*, our goal is to spread awareness of the biblical significance of the Land of Israel as well as the Jewish people's eternal connection to the land, based on the text of the *Tanakh*, the Hebrew Bible. We aim to honor "the God, the People and the Land of Israel" from an Orthodox Jewish perspective. To that end, *The Israel Bible* follows the traditional Jewish ordering of the books and the customary Hebrew division of chapters. Therefore, for example, we count 24 books of *Tanakh* with *Sefer Divrei Hayamim* (Chronicles) appearing last. It is our hope that our rich content will speak to all Jews and non-Jews who appreciate Israel as the God given land of the Jewish people.

English Translation – Throughout history, Jews have studied the Bible in Hebrew, as any form of translation would miss much of the nuance of the original holy tongue in which *Torah* has been transmitted since the days of Moses. However, as many Jews settled in America in the 19th Century, the need for an English translation became necessary. To be sure, there were already English translations prepared over the centuries by Christians, but in the words of the original editors of the Jewish Publication Society (JPS), "The Jew cannot afford to have his Bible translation prepared for him by others. He cannot have it as a gift, even as he cannot borrow his soul from others."

JPS set out in the late 1800s to publish an authoritative English translation "in the spirit of Jewish tradition." It was compiled over decades by some of the leading Jewish scholars of the time. They formed committees and subcommittees to compare existing English versions, considering medieval and modern Jewish commentators. The monumental JPS translation, originally published in 1917, has been updated in recent years, and *The Israel Bible* is proud to utilize the 1984 New Jewish Publication Society (NJPS) version with its modern, clear language, as well as its wide-ranging acceptance as an accurate and high-quality translation. We applied the NJPS translation verbatim, except for a select list of nouns which we replaced with their traditional Hebrew names. This is true even when we found the NJPS translation to be different than the popular translation of a word or phrase and when the NJPS switched the order of the text for the sake of clarity (see, for example, Ezekiel 24:22–24).

Hebrew Transliteration – To give our readers an authentic *Tanakh* experience, every verse that has commentary is transliterated from Hebrew into English. The Hebrew alphabet chart includes our standards for transliteration and pronunciation of Hebrew verses, enabling readers of *The Israel Bible* to decipher key biblical passages in the holy language. Readers can hear the entire Bible read in Hebrew on our website **www.theisraelbible.com**.

There are various standards when it comes to transliterating Hebrew words into English letters. While we have relied primarily on the classical Hebrew transliteration, we have occasionally deviated for the sake of simplicity, clarity and to reflect common usage.

In addition to whole verses, we have also transliterated many proper nouns in the English translation so that our readers can learn the names of key biblical figures and locations in their Hebrew form. As a rule, we chose to transliterate names of people that were central in the establishment and functioning of the nation of Israel, as well as significant places in the Holy Land. Therefore, regarding Adam's sons, for example, only *Shet* (Seth) is transliterated since it was from him that *Noach* (Noah), and ultimately *Avraham* (Abraham), descended. For this reason, there might be verses or sections of *The Israel Bible* that contains multiple names and only some of them are transliterated.

For the same reason, we have transliterated the names of the books of *Tanakh* when referring to them in our introductions and commentary. When referencing a specific chapter or verse, however, we use the English names of the books in our citations for clarity. We also transliterated ideas and concepts that are central to Judaism such as *Shabbat* (Sabbath), the names of the Jewish holidays and the *Beit Hamikdash* (Temple), as well as biblical measurements. Finally, the name of God is transliterated. Out of respect, Orthodox Jews generally refer to the Lord as *Hashem*, which literally means 'the Name.' Referring to God as *Hashem* reminds us that we feel close to Him but also recognize our distance at the same time. To stress this moniker, we transliterated both the Tetragrammaton as well as the name *Elohim* as *Hashem*.

Study Notes – Our unique commentary was compiled by Orthodox Jewish scholars who live in Israel. It is an anthology in the sense that most of the commentary is not original, but draws from traditional teachings of early Jewish Sages and modern rabbinic commentators. We also include quotations from individuals who have played a significant part in the past century of modern Israeli history including Israeli prime ministers, poets and military leaders.

Our commentary can be broken into four categories, three of which are identified by an icon at the beginning of the study note:

 Israel lessons are indicated with an icon bearing the map of Israel and focus on the Land of Israel and the modern State of Israel.

 Jewish lessons are indicated with a *Torah* scroll and teach a concept in Judaism or a classic idea from rabbinic thought.

 Hebrew lessons are represented by an icon bearing the letter *aleph* and focus on the meaning of a Hebrew word or phrase.

All other comments are considered general comments and are not assigned an icon.

Supplemental Material – In addition to our unique translation and original commentary, *The Israel Bible* offers supplementary material to enrich the learning experience of our readers. Before every book of *Tanakh*, we provide an introduction, as well as information, generally in the form of a map, a chart or a list, which is central to the specific book.

Maps – As the purpose of *The Israel Bible* is to highlight the biblical significance of the Land of Israel, significant time was spent researching and preparing maps to bring the physical contours of the holy land to life with great accuracy. However, since there is a lack of information regarding the precise locations of certain ancient cities, some of the places on our maps are approximate or subject to debate. In these cases, we followed the opinion that we are most comfortable with, but acknowledge that there is room for disagreement. We continue to produce new maps, which are available on our website **www.theisraelbible.com/maps**.

Torah **Readings** – The *Torah* is not just a work that is studied privately, it is also read out loud in synagogue. Every *Shabbat* and holiday a portion of the *Torah* is read, as well as a related section from *Neviim*, the prophets, called the *haftarah*. We included the blessings recited before and after the reading of the *Torah*, a list of the weekly *Torah* portions and their corresponding *haftarot*, and a chart of the *Torah* readings for special days with their corresponding *haftarot*. Readers can always find the current week's *Torah* portion by visiting **www.theisraelbible.com/weekly-torah-portion**. In this volume, we indicate where a new *Torah* portion begins by highlighting the Hebrew verse number with a gray box so readers can follow along with the communal *Torah* readings. Furthermore, we have included prayers for the State of Israel and the soldiers of the Israel Defense Forces (IDF) that are generally recited following the *Torah* reading in synagogue. It is our constant prayer that God watch over the State of Israel and the members of the IDF, who defend Israel every hour of every day.

In 1948, the State of Israel was created providing a modern answer to Isaiah's ancient question, "Is a nation born all at once?" (Isaiah 66:8). *The Israel Bible* was first published in the 70th year of God's miraculous restoration of the People of Israel to the Land of Israel. Jewish wisdom teaches that 70 is a significant number: *Moshe* (Moses) translated the *Torah* into 70 languages for all 70 nations of the world. From our very origins, the Jewish people were meant to be a light unto the 70 nations, spreading God's truth to the masses.

In the seven decades since the modern rebirth of the State of Israel, God's plan has been unfolding with unprecedented speed, dramatic highs and heartbreaking lows. Never has Israel been at the forefront of the world's attention as it is in our generation. Efforts to vilify the Jewish State seem to spread every day across the globe. At the same time, so does the growing movement of millions of non-Jewish biblical Zionists who stand with the nation of Israel as an expression of their commitment to God's word. As we seek to understand the clash of these two conflicting worldviews, the need for *The Israel Bible* has never been so important.

Standing on the great shoulders of those who came before us and emanating from the land that has always served as the birthplace for the Bible, we conclude with a heartfelt prayer: May the Almighty bless our efforts in offering this *Tanakh* to influence the hearts, minds and actions of its readers. In this way, it is our hope to spread God's name so that the publication of *The Israel Bible* brings us one step closer to the final redemption of Israel and the entire world.

Rabbi Tuly Weisz
Editor, *The Israel Bible*

Foreword

The mandate to study God's word daily is interestingly not found in the Five Books of Moses (Pentateuch), but rather in the first book of our prophetic writings: "Let not this Book of the Teaching cease from your lips, but recite it day and night, so that you may observe faithfully all that is written in it. Only then will you prosper in your undertakings and only then will you be successful" (Joshua 1:8). Charged with bringing the Israelites into the land covenantally promised to Abraham, Isaac and Jacob, God ensures Joshua of His protection if the nation observes His ways as dictated in the Divine constitution known as the *Torah*.

In Jewish tradition, Joshua (1:8) is directly linked with Deuteronomy (11:14), "You shall gather in your new grain and wine, and oil."[1] Our Sages deduced from this scriptural combination the importance of merging *Torah* study with a profession. Completely dedicating oneself to the study of *Torah* without having the financial means to sustain this lifestyle can lead one to eventually straying from observance of God's will. Poverty and crime can have an intimate relationship.

We must also be careful that our work does not affect our daily study of Scripture. The addiction of becoming a workaholic and not making *Torah* study a priority can also lead one into temptations that can violate our personal relationship with Him as well as our fellow human beings. The goal is to achieve a healthy balance between our study of God's word and our daily work.

The Deuteronomic verse quoted above is part of the second section of the Shema[2] that discusses the concept of reward and punishment. Sanctifying God by fulfilling His commandments results in the Land of Israel practically benefitting from rains that occur in the right season and reaping the abundance from the fields. However, if the nation follows pagan gods and practices, the consequences are devastating – famine and death. The Land of Israel is intrinsically linked with the keeping of the *Torah*. Covenant Land comes with covenant responsibility.

---

1 Talmud Bavli Berachot 35b

2 Consisting of three sections within the Five Books of Moses (Deut. 6:4–8; 11:13–22 and Numbers 15:37–42), the *Shema* is proclamation of accepting God's Kingdom in our lives, loyalty to His commandments and remembering His redemptive act of liberating us from Egypt. Jews recite the *Shema* twice a day as stated in Deut. 6:7.

Born into slavery, Joshua is now leading His people into the Promised Land. More than 500 years separates him from his ancestral forefather Abraham. The historical narratives that took place between Abraham leaving everything behind to follow God in Genesis 12 and the death of Moses in the last chapter of Deuteronomy are filled with intrigue, suspense, joy, sorrow and hope. What began as a family is now a nation actualizing its mission to be a kingdom of priests to the world. However, for the Israelites to succeed in the Land of Israel, they must see the *Torah* as the only compass to direct their lives.

The biblical episodes after our first entry into the land are well known. Our ancestors' triumphs and sins are all on public record. We learned the harsh reality of Leviticus (18:28) "So let not the land spew you out for defiling it as it spewed out the nation that came before you." Twice, we lost the privilege to be stewards of the Land of Israel and to fulfill our nation state mandate to be a light to the world. However, when the annals of history were ready to archive the Jewish people after the Holocaust, God kept His covenantal promise and gathered us from the four corners of the globe to come home. The year 1948 was a game changer. Biblical prophecies were and are being realized. We are now living in the birth pangs of the messianic era.

In our morning prayers, we recite a series of blessings over the *Torah* that include petitioning God to have a sweet tooth for His word, to study it without any ulterior motive and to have Him to teach it to us. They are some congregations that invoke the following liturgical prayer after the completion of these blessings: *May the Torah be my faith and El Shaddai my help. Blessed be the name of His glorious kingdom forever and all time.*

According to Jewish tradition, the neglect of not blessing the *Torah* before engaging in its study was one of the reasons for the destruction of the Temple.[3] This is deduced from the redundancy of words in Jeremiah (9:12) that talks about Israel not following God: "…Because they forsook the teaching I had set before them. They did not obey Me and they did not follow it [did not make a blessing before studying it]." Our inability to properly cherish God's greatest gift to the world, the *Torah*, led to our eventual exile from our land.

On Israel's Independence Day, Jews around the world recite Psalms 113–118 to express our gratitude to God for His Divine hand in helping establish the State of Israel. We have learned from our past and realize the privilege to see firsthand the land, people and *Torah* operating all together in our generation.

---

3   Babylonian Talmud Nedarim 81a

When Rabbi Tuly Weisz approached me about his intent to publish *The Israel Bible* that would highlight commentary about the special relationship between the land and people, I saw this project as another way to publicly demonstrate our appreciation to God for having the State of Israel. In addition, it is another educational tool to ensure biblical literacy. If we are to truly enjoy the Land of Israel, it is incumbent upon us to continually study the *Torah*. Isaiah once prophesied that the Jewish people would return to Zion with songs, "crowned with everlasting joy" (35:10). *The Israel Bible* provides us the lyrical content to express our joy in living in the land that God calls holy.

Rabbi Shlomo Riskin
Chief Rabbi of Efrat
Founder of the Center for Jewish-Christian
Understanding & Cooperation (cjcuc)

Sefer Daniel
The Book of Daniel

Introduction and commentary by Batya Markowitz

Sefer Daniel (Daniel) is the story of the People of Israel in exile, longing to return to the Land of Israel. Much of the book is even written in Aramaic, the language that was spoken in Babylonia during the seventy years of exile following the destruction of the first *Beit Hamikdash*.

The book opens with the exile of *Daniel* and his contemporaries from the Holy Land to Babylonia. There, he and his contemporaries are chosen to serve in Nebuchadnezzar's court. When *Daniel* succeeds at interpreting the king's dream, he is promoted to a high position. *Daniel* serves in the royal court throughout the reign of Nebuchadnezzar, until the downfall of Babylonia in the days of Belshazzar, Nebuchadnezzar's grandson, and retains a position of power even when Darius of Media ascends the throne.

Daniel is an extremely righteous and talented leader. When Darius's officials try to incriminate him, "they could find neither fault nor corruption, inasmuch as he was trustworthy, and no negligence or corruption was to be found in him" (Daniel 6:5). Throughout the second half of the book, *Daniel* mourns the destruction of the Temple and all the exiles that the Jews are to experience, and grieves over all the suffering they bring with them.

Sefer Daniel tells of the dangers, both physical and spiritual, encountered in the exile in foreign lands. Throughout the book, various attempts are made to sever the Jews' connection with their God and their land. *Chananya*, *Mishael* and *Azarya* are thrown into a furnace when they refuse to worship Nebuchadnezzar's idol. *Daniel* is thrown into a lions' den when he continues to pray to *Hashem* in violation of the king's decree. These righteous leaders are saved miraculously each time, showing the Jews that God has not abandoned them. This reassures the Jewish people that they are still connected to *Hashem* despite the exile, and that they will one day return to *Eretz Yisrael* as He promised.

The book is full of visions regarding the first exile, Nebuchadnezzar's reign, and all subsequent exiles until the arrival of the *Mashiach*. The Jews in exile are encouraged when they see that Nebuchadnezzar receives divine retribution for having destroyed *Yerushalayim* and the *Beit Hamikdash*. They see that the words of the prophets are indeed fulfilled when Babylonia's rule is terminated suddenly after seventy years, just as *Yirmiyahu* had predicted before they left the Land of Israel (Jeremiah 29:10). In the middle of a feast celebrating the fact that *Hashem* has forsaken the Jews in this foreign land, Belshazzar sees the "writing on the wall," showing that God has indeed calculated the seventy years, and that Babylon will be overrun by the Persian and Median empires.

The second half of the book is made up of the prophetic visions that *Daniel* received during this period. The visions are graphic and often ominous, foretelling the future exiles and suffering that the Jewish people will endure. At the same time, they are vague and obscure, allowing for various interpretations.

The medieval scholar Rabbi Yehuda Halevi writes in his philosophical work *The Kuzari*, that as a general rule, prophecy can only be received in *Eretz Yisrael*. *Daniel*, however, was able to receive prophetic visions in Babylonia because they were about, and for the sake of, *Eretz Yisrael*. They foretold the return of the Children of Israel to their homeland in the time of the second *Beit Hamikdash*, as well as their ultimate return at the end of days. These prophecies encouraged *Daniel* and the Jews of his generation, and they continue to serve as an encouragement that the God of Israel is a keeper of promises.

Throughout history, the People of Israel have been persecuted in foreign lands. *Sefer Daniel* is a study of Jewish survival in exile and the ultimate redemption.

Chart of the 70 Years of Babylonian Exile

It is well known that the Babylonian exile lasted 70 years. In fact, there were two sets of 70 years associated with the Babylonian exile and the destruction of the *Beit Hamikdash*. The following chart presents the two sets of 70 years and the relevant biblical verses relating to each. It is followed by a more detailed explanation.

70 Years	Beginning	End	Verse
Babylonian rule	605 BCE – Nebuchadnezzar defeats the Assyrians and Egyptians at the battle of Carchemish and then takes control of *Yehuda*.	538 BCE – The Babylonians fall to the Persians	Jeremiah 25:11 – And those nations shall serve the king of Babylon seventy years Ezra 1:1 – In the first year of King Cyrus of Persia, when the word of *Hashem* spoken by *Yirmiyahu* was fulfilled
Destruction of Yerushalayim	586 BCE – Destruction of *Yerushalayim* and the *Beit Hamikdash*	516 BCE – Construction of the second *Beit Hamikdash* is completed.	Jeremiah 29:10 – I will take note of you, and I will fulfill to you My promise of favor – to bring you back to this place Daniel 9:2 – the term of *Yerushalayim*'s desolation – seventy years

Sefer Daniel takes place during the Babylonian exile, which *Yirmiyahu* had predicted would last seventy years:

"This whole land shall be a desolate ruin. And those nations shall serve the king of Babylon seventy years. When the seventy years are over, I will punish the king of Babylon and that nation and the land of the Chaldeans for their sins – declares *Hashem* – and I will make it a desolation for all time" (Jeremiah 25:11–12).

"For thus said *Hashem*: When Babylon's seventy years are over, I will take note of you, and I will fulfill to you My promise of favor – to bring you back to this place" (Jeremiah 29:10).

Chapter 9 of *Sefer Daniel* starts with *Daniel*'s attempt to calculate the seventy years of Babylonian exile prophesied by the prophet *Yirmiyahu*:

"I, Daniel, consulted the books concerning the number of years that, according to the word of *Hashem* that had come to *Yirmiyahu* the prophet, were to be the term of *Yerushalayim*'s desolation – seventy years" (Daniel 9:2).

Many commentators, for example *Malbim*, explain that there were actually two different sets of seventy years. The first refers to seventy years of Babylonian reign. This began in the year 605 BCE, the fourth year of King *Yehoyakim*, when Nebuchadnezzar defeated the Assyrians and Egyptians in the battle at Carchemish and the Babylonians became the ruling world power, seizing control of *Yehuda* (see Jeremiah 25:1). It ended with the fall of the Babylonians to the Persians in 538 BCE. This understanding of the seventy years, as referring to seventy years of Babylonian rule, is reflected in the words of *Sefer Yirmiyahu* (25:11): "And those nations shall serve the king of Babylon seventy years." This also explains the first verse in *Sefer Ezra* which says "In the first year of King Cyrus of Persia, when the word of *Hashem* spoken by *Yirmiyahu* was fulfilled…" The defeat of the Babylonians by Cyrus of Persia marked the end of the seventy years of *Yirmiyahu*'s prophecy. Indeed, there were just about seventy years between the time that Nebuchadnezzar took control of *Yehuda* (605 BCE) until the Babylonia fell to the Persians (538 BCE). There are a number of ways of explaining the missing 3 years which are beyond the scope of this paragraph, but the simplest explanation is that the Bible often speaks in round numbers.

The second set of seventy years refers to the destruction of *Yerushalayim* and the *Beit Hamikdash*. This, according to the *Malbim*, is what *Daniel* was referring to when he said: "the term of *Yerushalayim*'s desolation – seventy years." He says that this understanding of 70 years is reflected in the words of *Yirmiyahu* (29:10): "I will take note of you, and I will fulfill to you My promise of favor – to bring you back to this place." The amount of time that passed from the destruction of *Yerushalayim* and the first *Beit Hamikdash* in 586 BCE, until the completion of the reconstruction of the second *Beit Hamikdash* in the sixth year of King Darius, 516 BCE, was indeed seventy years.

1 ¹ In the third year of the reign of King *Yehoyakim* of *Yehuda*, King Nebuchadnezzar of Babylon came to *Yerushalayim* and laid siege to it.

א בִּשְׁנַת שָׁלוֹשׁ לְמַלְכוּת יְהוֹיָקִים מֶלֶךְ־יְהוּדָה בָּא נְבוּכַדְנֶאצַּר מֶלֶךְ־בָּבֶל יְרוּשָׁלַﬦִ וַיָּצַר עָלֶיהָ:

² *Hashem* delivered King *Yehoyakim* of *Yehuda* into his power, together with some of the vessels of the House of *Hashem*, and he brought them to the land of Shinar to the house of his god; he deposited the vessels in the treasury of his god.

ב וַיִּתֵּן אֲדֹנָי בְּיָדוֹ אֶת־יְהוֹיָקִים מֶלֶךְ־יְהוּדָה וּמִקְצָת כְּלֵי בֵית־הָאֱלֹהִים וַיְבִיאֵם אֶרֶץ־שִׁנְעָר בֵּית אֱלֹהָיו וְאֶת־הַכֵּלִים הֵבִיא בֵּית אוֹצַר אֱלֹהָיו:

va-yi-TAYN a-do-NAI b'-ya-DO et y'-ho-ya-KEEM ME-lekh y'-hu-DAH u-mik-TZAT k'-LAY vayt ha-e-lo-HEEM vai-vee-AYM E-retz shin-AR BAYT e-lo-HAV v'-et ha-kay-LEEM hay-VEE BAYT o-TZAR e-lo-HAV

³ Then the king ordered Ashpenaz, his chief officer, to bring some Israelites of royal descent and of the nobility –

ג וַיֹּאמֶר הַמֶּלֶךְ לְאַשְׁפְּנַז רַב סָרִיסָיו לְהָבִיא מִבְּנֵי יִשְׂרָאֵל וּמִזֶּרַע הַמְּלוּכָה וּמִן־הַפַּרְתְּמִים:

⁴ youths without blemish, handsome, proficient in all wisdom, knowledgeable and intelligent, and capable of serving in the royal palace – and teach them the writings and the language of the Chaldeans.

ד יְלָדִים אֲשֶׁר אֵין־בָּהֶם כָּל־מאוּם [מוּם] וְטוֹבֵי מַרְאֶה וּמַשְׂכִּילִים בְּכָל־חָכְמָה וְיֹדְעֵי דַעַת וּמְבִינֵי מַדָּע וַאֲשֶׁר כֹּחַ בָּהֶם לַעֲמֹד בְּהֵיכַל הַמֶּלֶךְ וּלְלַמְּדָם סֵפֶר וּלְשׁוֹן כַּשְׂדִּים:

⁵ The king allotted daily rations to them from the king's food and from the wine he drank. They were to be educated for three years, at the end of which they were to enter the king's service.

ה וַיְמַן לָהֶם הַמֶּלֶךְ דְּבַר־יוֹם בְּיוֹמוֹ מִפַּת־בַּג הַמֶּלֶךְ וּמִיֵּין מִשְׁתָּיו וּלְגַדְּלָם שָׁנִים שָׁלוֹשׁ וּמִקְצָתָם יַעַמְדוּ לִפְנֵי הַמֶּלֶךְ:

⁶ Among them were the Judahites *Daniel*, *Chananya*, *Mishael* and *Azarya*.

ו וַיְהִי בָהֶם מִבְּנֵי יְהוּדָה דָּנִיֵּאל חֲנַנְיָה מִישָׁאֵל וַעֲזַרְיָה:

⁷ The chief officer gave them new names; he named *Daniel* Belteshazzar, *Chananya* Shadrach, *Mishael* Meshach, and *Azarya* Abed-nego.

ז וַיָּשֶׂם לָהֶם שַׂר הַסָּרִיסִים שֵׁמוֹת וַיָּשֶׂם לְדָנִיֵּאל בֵּלְטְשַׁאצַּר וְלַחֲנַנְיָה שַׁדְרַךְ וּלְמִישָׁאֵל מֵישַׁךְ וְלַעֲזַרְיָה עֲבֵד נְגוֹ:

⁸ *Daniel* resolved not to defile himself with the king's food or the wine he drank, so he sought permission of the chief officer not to defile himself,

ח וַיָּשֶׂם דָּנִיֵּאל עַל־לִבּוֹ אֲשֶׁר לֹא־יִתְגָּאַל בְּפַתְבַּג הַמֶּלֶךְ וּבְיֵין מִשְׁתָּיו וַיְבַקֵּשׁ מִשַּׂר הַסָּרִיסִים אֲשֶׁר לֹא יִתְגָּאָל:

Sunburst over the Old City of *Yerushalayim*

1:2 *Hashem* **delivered King** *Yehoyakim* **of** *Yehuda* **into his power** The exile from the Land of Israel to Babylonia happened in three stages. In the first stage, Nebuchadnezzar, king of Babylonia, deported King *Yehoyakim*, some young Judeans, and vessels from the *Beit Hamikdash*. *Hashem* hoped that the People of Israel would be shaken after this calamitous event, and that they would repent and avert further punishment. Unfortunately, the people ignored this message and were eventually exiled in two additional stages. The young Jews who arrived first in Babylonia were ultimately able to encourage their brothers who came in the subsequent rounds of exile. When the later stages of exile arrived, they found *Daniel*, *Chananya*, *Mishael*, and *Azarya*, in positions of power in the palace. This gave them the strength to survive, avoid assimilation, and not to despair of their eventual return to *Eretz Yisrael*.

9 and *Hashem* disposed the chief officer to be kind and compassionate toward *Daniel*.

ט וַיִּתֵּן הָאֱלֹהִים אֶת־דָּנִיֵּאל לְחֶסֶד וּלְרַחֲמִים לִפְנֵי שַׂר הַסָּרִיסִים:

10 The chief officer said to *Daniel*, "I fear that my lord the king, who allotted food and drink to you, will notice that you look out of sorts, unlike the other youths of your age – and you will put my life in jeopardy with the king."

י וַיֹּאמֶר שַׂר הַסָּרִיסִים לְדָנִיֵּאל יָרֵא אֲנִי אֶת־אֲדֹנִי הַמֶּלֶךְ אֲשֶׁר מִנָּה אֶת־מַאֲכַלְכֶם וְאֶת־מִשְׁתֵּיכֶם אֲשֶׁר לָמָּה יִרְאֶה אֶת־פְּנֵיכֶם זֹעֲפִים מִן־הַיְלָדִים אֲשֶׁר כְּגִילְכֶם וְחִיַּבְתֶּם אֶת־רֹאשִׁי לַמֶּלֶךְ:

11 *Daniel* replied to the guard whom the chief officer had put in charge of *Daniel, Chananya, Mishael* and *Azarya,*

יא וַיֹּאמֶר דָּנִיֵּאל אֶל־הַמֶּלְצַר אֲשֶׁר מִנָּה שַׂר הַסָּרִיסִים עַל־דָּנִיֵּאל חֲנַנְיָה מִישָׁאֵל וַעֲזַרְיָה:

12 "Please test your servants for ten days, giving us legumes to eat and water to drink.

יב נַס־נָא אֶת־עֲבָדֶיךָ יָמִים עֲשָׂרָה וְיִתְּנוּ־לָנוּ מִן־הַזֵּרֹעִים וְנֹאכְלָה וּמַיִם וְנִשְׁתֶּה:

13 Then compare our appearance with that of the youths who eat of the king's food, and do with your servants as you see fit."

יג וְיֵרָאוּ לְפָנֶיךָ מַרְאֵינוּ וּמַרְאֵה הַיְלָדִים הָאֹכְלִים אֵת פַּתְבַּג הַמֶּלֶךְ וְכַאֲשֶׁר תִּרְאֵה עֲשֵׂה עִם־עֲבָדֶיךָ:

14 He agreed to this plan of theirs, and tested them for ten days.

יד וַיִּשְׁמַע לָהֶם לַדָּבָר הַזֶּה וַיְנַסֵּם יָמִים עֲשָׂרָה:

15 When the ten days were over, they looked better and healthier than all the youths who were eating of the king's food.

טו וּמִקְצָת יָמִים עֲשָׂרָה נִרְאָה מַרְאֵיהֶם טוֹב וּבְרִיאֵי בָּשָׂר מִן־כָּל־הַיְלָדִים הָאֹכְלִים אֵת פַּתְבַּג הַמֶּלֶךְ:

16 So the guard kept on removing their food, and the wine they were supposed to drink, and gave them legumes.

טז וַיְהִי הַמֶּלְצַר נֹשֵׂא אֶת־פַּתְבָּגָם וְיֵין מִשְׁתֵּיהֶם וְנֹתֵן לָהֶם זֵרֹעֲנִים:

17 *Hashem* made all four of these young men intelligent and proficient in all writings and wisdom, and *Daniel* had understanding of visions and dreams of all kinds.

יז וְהַיְלָדִים הָאֵלֶּה אַרְבַּעְתָּם נָתַן לָהֶם הָאֱלֹהִים מַדָּע וְהַשְׂכֵּל בְּכָל־סֵפֶר וְחָכְמָה וְדָנִיֵּאל הֵבִין בְּכָל־חָזוֹן וַחֲלֹמוֹת:

18 When the time the king had set for their presentation had come, the chief officer presented them to Nebuchadnezzar.

יח וּלְמִקְצָת הַיָּמִים אֲשֶׁר־אָמַר הַמֶּלֶךְ לַהֲבִיאָם וַיְבִיאֵם שַׂר הַסָּרִיסִים לִפְנֵי נְבֻכַדְנֶצַּר:

19 The king spoke with them, and of them all none was equal to *Daniel, Chananya, Mishael* and *Azarya;* so these entered the king's service.

יט וַיְדַבֵּר אִתָּם הַמֶּלֶךְ וְלֹא נִמְצָא מִכֻּלָּם כְּדָנִיֵּאל חֲנַנְיָה מִישָׁאֵל וַעֲזַרְיָה וַיַּעַמְדוּ לִפְנֵי הַמֶּלֶךְ:

20 Whenever the king put a question to them requiring wisdom and understanding, he found them to be ten times better than all the magicians and exorcists throughout his realm.

כ וְכֹל דְּבַר חָכְמַת בִּינָה אֲשֶׁר־בִּקֵּשׁ מֵהֶם הַמֶּלֶךְ וַיִּמְצָאֵם עֶשֶׂר יָדוֹת עַל כָּל־הַחַרְטֻמִּים הָאַשָּׁפִים אֲשֶׁר בְּכָל־מַלְכוּתוֹ:

21 *Daniel* was there until the first year of King Cyrus.

כא וַיְהִי דָּנִיֵּאל עַד־שְׁנַת אַחַת לְכוֹרֶשׁ הַמֶּלֶךְ:

Daniel

2

2 ¹ In the second year of the reign of Nebuchadnezzar, Nebuchadnezzar had a dream; his spirit was agitated, yet he was overcome by sleep.

ב א וּבִשְׁנַת שְׁתַּיִם לְמַלְכוּת נְבֻכַדְנֶצַּר חָלַם נְבֻכַדְנֶצַּר חֲלֹמוֹת וַתִּתְפָּעֶם רוּחוֹ וּשְׁנָתוֹ נִהְיְתָה עָלָיו:

² The king ordered the magicians, exorcists, sorcerers, and Chaldeans to be summoned in order to tell the king what he had dreamed. They came and stood before the king,

ב וַיֹּאמֶר הַמֶּלֶךְ לִקְרֹא לַחַרְטֻמִּים וְלָאַשָּׁפִים וְלַמְכַשְּׁפִים וְלַכַּשְׂדִּים לְהַגִּיד לַמֶּלֶךְ חֲלֹמֹתָיו וַיָּבֹאוּ וַיַּעַמְדוּ לִפְנֵי הַמֶּלֶךְ:

³ and the king said to them, "I have had a dream and I am full of anxiety to know what I have dreamed."

ג וַיֹּאמֶר לָהֶם הַמֶּלֶךְ חֲלוֹם חָלָמְתִּי וַתִּפָּעֶם רוּחִי לָדַעַת אֶת־הַחֲלוֹם:

⁴ The Chaldeans spoke to the king in Aramaic, "O king, live forever! Relate the dream to your servants, and we will tell its meaning."

ד וַיְדַבְּרוּ הַכַּשְׂדִּים לַמֶּלֶךְ אֲרָמִית מַלְכָּא לְעָלְמִין חֱיִי אֱמַר חֶלְמָא לעבדיך [לְעַבְדָךְ] וּפִשְׁרָא נְחַוֵּא:

⁵ The king said in reply to the Chaldeans, "I hereby decree: If you will not make the dream and its meaning known to me, you shall be torn limb from limb and your houses confiscated.

ה עָנֵה מַלְכָּא וְאָמַר לכשדיא [לְכַשְׂדָּאֵי] מִלְּתָא מִנִּי אַזְדָּא הֵן לָא תְהוֹדְעוּנַּנִי חֶלְמָא וּפִשְׁרֵהּ הַדָּמִין תִּתְעַבְדוּן וּבָתֵּיכוֹן נְוָלִי יִתְּשָׂמוּן:

⁶ But if you tell the dream and its meaning, you shall receive from me gifts, presents, and great honor; therefore, tell me the dream and its meaning."

ו וְהֵן חֶלְמָא וּפִשְׁרֵהּ תְּהַחֲוֹן מַתְּנָן וּנְבִזְבָּה וִיקָר שַׂגִּיא תְּקַבְּלוּן מִן־קֳדָמָי לָהֵן חֶלְמָא וּפִשְׁרֵהּ הַחֲוֹנִי:

⁷ Once again they answered, "Let the king relate the dream to his servants, and we will tell its meaning."

ז עֲנוֹ תִנְיָנוּת וְאָמְרִין מַלְכָּא חֶלְמָא יֵאמַר לְעַבְדוֹהִי וּפִשְׁרָה נְהַחֲוֵה:

⁸ The king said in reply, "It is clear to me that you are playing for time, since you see that I have decreed

ח עָנֵה מַלְכָּא וְאָמַר מִן־יַצִּיב יָדַע אֲנָה דִּי עִדָּנָא אַנְתּוּן זָבְנִין כָּל־קֳבֵל דִּי חֲזֵיתוֹן דִּי אַזְדָּא מִנִּי מִלְּתָא:

⁹ that if you do not make the dream known to me, there is but one verdict for you. You have conspired to tell me something false and fraudulent until circumstances change; so relate the dream to me, and I will then know that you can tell its meaning."

ט דִּי הֵן חֶלְמָא לָא תְהוֹדְעֻנַּנִי חֲדָה־הִיא דָתְכוֹן וּמִלָּה כִדְבָה וּשְׁחִיתָה הזמנתון [הִזְדְּמִנְתּוּן] לְמֵאמַר קָדָמַי עַד דִּי עִדָּנָא יִשְׁתַּנֵּא לָהֵן חֶלְמָא אֱמַרוּ לִי וְאִנְדַּע דִּי פִשְׁרֵהּ תְּהַחֲוֻנַּנִי:

¹⁰ The Chaldeans said in reply to the king, "There is no one on earth who can satisfy the king's demand, for great king or ruler – none has ever asked such a thing of any magician, exorcist, or Chaldean.

י עֲנוֹ כשדיא [כַשְׂדָּאֵי] קֳדָם־מַלְכָּא וְאָמְרִין לָא־אִיתַי אֱנָשׁ עַל־יַבֶּשְׁתָּא דִּי מִלַּת מַלְכָּא יוּכַל לְהַחֲוָיָה כָּל־קֳבֵל דִּי כָּל־מֶלֶךְ רַב וְשַׁלִּיט מִלָּה כִדְנָה לָא שְׁאֵל לְכָל־חַרְטֹם וְאָשַׁף וְכַשְׂדָּי:

¹¹ The thing asked by the king is difficult; there is no one who can tell it to the king except the gods whose abode is not among mortals."

יא וּמִלְּתָא דִי־מַלְכָּה שָׁאֵל יַקִּירָה וְאָחֳרָן לָא אִיתַי דִּי יְחַוִּנַּהּ קֳדָם מַלְכָּא לָהֵן אֱלָהִין דִּי מְדָרְהוֹן עִם־בִּשְׂרָא לָא אִיתוֹהִי:

¹² Whereupon the king flew into a violent rage, and gave an order to do away with all the wise men of Babylon.

יב כָּל־קֳבֵל דְּנָה מַלְכָּא בְּנַס וּקְצַף שַׂגִּיא וַאֲמַר לְהוֹבָדָה לְכֹל חַכִּימֵי בָבֶל:

13 The decree condemning the wise men to death was issued. *Daniel* and his companions were about to be put to death

יג וְדָתָא נֶפְקַת וְחַכִּימַיָּא מִתְקַטְּלִין וּבְעוֹ דָּנִיֵּאל וְחַבְרוֹהִי לְהִתְקְטָלָה:

14 when *Daniel* remonstrated with Arioch, the captain of the royal guard who had set out to put the wise men of Babylon to death.

יד בֵּאדַיִן דָּנִיֵּאל הֲתִיב עֵטָא וּטְעֵם לְאַרְיוֹךְ רַב־טַבָּחַיָּא דִּי מַלְכָּא דִּי נְפַק לְקַטָּלָה לְחַכִּימֵי בָּבֶל:

15 He spoke up and said to Arioch, the royal officer, "Why is the decree of the king so urgent?" Thereupon Arioch informed *Daniel* of the matter.

טו עָנֵה וְאָמַר לְאַרְיוֹךְ שַׁלִּיטָא דִּי־מַלְכָּא עַל־מָה דָתָא מְהַחְצְפָה מִן־קֳדָם מַלְכָּא אֱדַיִן מִלְּתָא הוֹדַע אַרְיוֹךְ לְדָנִיֵּאל:

16 So *Daniel* went to ask the king for time, that he might tell the meaning to the king.

טז וְדָנִיֵּאל עַל וּבְעָה מִן־מַלְכָּא דִּי זְמָן יִנְתֶּן־לֵהּ וּפִשְׁרָא לְהַחֲוָיָה לְמַלְכָּא:

17 Then *Daniel* went to his house and informed his companions, *Chananya, Mishael,* and *Azarya,* of the matter,

יז אֱדַיִן דָּנִיֵּאל לְבַיְתֵהּ אֲזַל וְלַחֲנַנְיָה מִישָׁאֵל וַעֲזַרְיָה חַבְרוֹהִי מִלְּתָא הוֹדַע:

18 that they might implore the God of Heaven for help regarding this mystery, so that *Daniel* and his colleagues would not be put to death together with the other wise men of Babylon.

יח וְרַחֲמִין לְמִבְעֵא מִן־קֳדָם אֱלָהּ שְׁמַיָּא עַל־רָזָה דְּנָה דִּי לָא יְהֹבְדוּן דָּנִיֵּאל וְחַבְרוֹהִי עִם־שְׁאָר חַכִּימֵי בָבֶל:

19 The mystery was revealed to *Daniel* in a night vision; then *Daniel* blessed the God of Heaven.

יט אֱדַיִן לְדָנִיֵּאל בְּחֶזְוָא דִי־לֵילְיָא רָזָה גֲלִי אֱדַיִן דָּנִיֵּאל בָּרִךְ לֶאֱלָהּ שְׁמַיָּא:

20 *Daniel* spoke up and said: "Let the name of *Hashem* be blessed forever and ever, For wisdom and power are His.

כ עָנֵה דָנִיֵּאל וְאָמַר לֶהֱוֵא שְׁמֵהּ דִּי־אֱלָהָא מְבָרַךְ מִן־עָלְמָא וְעַד־עָלְמָא דִּי חָכְמְתָא וּגְבוּרְתָא דִּי לֵהּ־הִיא:

21 He changes times and seasons, Removes kings and installs kings; He gives the wise their wisdom And knowledge to those who know.

כא וְהוּא מְהַשְׁנֵא עִדָּנַיָּא וְזִמְנַיָּא מְהַעְדֵּה מַלְכִין וּמְהָקֵים מַלְכִין יָהֵב חָכְמְתָא לְחַכִּימִין וּמַנְדְּעָא לְיָדְעֵי בִינָה:

22 He reveals deep and hidden things, Knows what is in the darkness, And light dwells with Him.

כב הוּא גָּלֵא עַמִּיקָתָא וּמְסַתְּרָתָא יָדַע מָה בַחֲשׁוֹכָא וּנְהִירָא [וּנְהוֹרָא] עִמֵּהּ שְׁרֵא:

23 I acknowledge and praise You, O God of my fathers, You who have given me wisdom and power, For now You have let me know what we asked of You; You have let us know what concerns the king."

כג לָךְ אֱלָהּ אֲבָהָתִי מְהוֹדֵא וּמְשַׁבַּח אֲנָה דִּי חָכְמְתָא וּגְבוּרְתָא יְהַבְתְּ לִי וּכְעַן הוֹדַעְתַּנִי דִּי־בְעֵינָא מִנָּךְ דִּי־מִלַּת מַלְכָּא הוֹדַעְתֶּנָא:

24 Thereupon *Daniel* went to Arioch, whom the king had appointed to do away with the wise men of Babylon; he came and said to him as follows, "Do not do away with the wise men of Babylon; bring me to the king and I will tell the king the meaning!"

כד כָּל־קֳבֵל דְּנָה דָּנִיֵּאל עַל עַל־אַרְיוֹךְ דִּי מַנִּי מַלְכָּא לְהוֹבָדָה לְחַכִּימֵי בָבֶל אֲזַל וְכֵן אֲמַר־לֵהּ לְחַכִּימֵי בָבֶל אַל־תְּהוֹבֵד הַעֵלְנִי קֳדָם מַלְכָּא וּפִשְׁרָא לְמַלְכָּא אֲחַוֵּא:

25 So Arioch rushed *Daniel* into the king's presence and said to him, "I have found among the exiles of *Yehuda* a man who can make the meaning known to the king!"

כה אֱדַיִן אַרְיוֹךְ בְּהִתְבְּהָלָה הַנְעֵל לְדָנִיֵּאל קֳדָם מַלְכָּא וְכֵן אֲמַר־לֵהּ דִּי־הַשְׁכַּחַת גְּבַר מִן־בְּנֵי גָלוּתָא דִּי יְהוּד דִּי פִשְׁרָא לְמַלְכָּא יְהוֹדַע:

²⁶ The king said in reply to *Daniel* (who was called Belteshazzar), "Can you really make known to me the dream that I saw and its meaning?"

עָנֵה מַלְכָּא וְאָמַר לְדָנִיֵּאל דִּי שְׁמֵהּ בֵּלְטְשַׁאצַּר הַאִיתָיךְ [הַאִיתָךְ] כָּהֵל לְהוֹדָעֻתַנִי חֶלְמָא דִי־חֲזֵית וּפִשְׁרֵהּ: כו

²⁷ *Daniel* answered the king and said, "The mystery about which the king has inquired – wise men, exorcists, magicians, and diviners cannot tell to the king.

עָנֵה דָנִיֵּאל קֳדָם מַלְכָּא וְאָמַר רָזָה דִּי־מַלְכָּא שָׁאֵל לָא חַכִּימִין אָשְׁפִין חַרְטֻמִּין גָּזְרִין יָכְלִין לְהַחֲוָיָה לְמַלְכָּא: כז

²⁸ But there is a *Hashem* in heaven who reveals mysteries, and He has made known to King Nebuchadnezzar what is to be at the end of days. This is your dream and the vision that entered your mind in bed:

בְּרַם אִיתַי אֱלָהּ בִּשְׁמַיָּא גָּלֵא רָזִין וְהוֹדַע לְמַלְכָּא נְבוּכַדְנֶצַּר מָה דִּי לֶהֱוֵא בְּאַחֲרִית יוֹמַיָּא חֶלְמָךְ וְחֶזְוֵי רֵאשָׁךְ עַל־מִשְׁכְּבָךְ דְּנָה הוּא: כח

²⁹ O king, the thoughts that came to your mind in your bed are about future events; He who reveals mysteries has let you know what is to happen.

אַנְתְּ מַלְכָּא רַעְיוֹנָךְ עַל־מִשְׁכְּבָךְ סְלִקוּ מָה דִּי לֶהֱוֵא אַחֲרֵי דְנָה וְגָלֵא רָזַיָּא הוֹדְעָךְ מָה־דִי לֶהֱוֵא: כט

³⁰ Not because my wisdom is greater than that of other creatures has this mystery been revealed to me, but in order that the meaning should be made known to the king, and that you may know the thoughts of your mind.

וַאֲנָה לָא בְחָכְמָה דִּי־אִיתַי בִּי מִן־כָּל־חַיַּיָּא רָזָא דְנָה גֱּלִי לִי לָהֵן עַל־דִּבְרַת דִּי פִשְׁרָא לְמַלְכָּא יְהוֹדְעוּן וְרַעְיוֹנֵי לִבְבָךְ תִּנְדַּע: ל

³¹ "O king, as you looked on, there appeared a great statue. This statue, which was huge and its brightness surpassing, stood before you, and its appearance was awesome.

אַנְתְּ מַלְכָּא חָזֵה הֲוַיְתָ וַאֲלוּ צְלֵם חַד שַׂגִּיא צַלְמָא דִּכֵּן רַב וְזִיוֵהּ יַתִּיר קָאֵם לְקָבְלָךְ וְרֵוֵהּ דְּחִיל: לא

³² The head of that statue was of fine gold; its breast and arms were of silver; its belly and thighs, of bronze;

הוּא צַלְמָא רֵאשֵׁהּ דִּי־דְהַב טָב חֲדוֹהִי וּדְרָעוֹהִי דִּי כְסַף מְעוֹהִי וְיַרְכָתֵהּ דִּי נְחָשׁ: לב

³³ its legs were of iron, and its feet part iron and part clay.

שָׁקוֹהִי דִּי פַרְזֶל רַגְלוֹהִי מנהון [מִנְּהֵין] דִּי פַרְזֶל ומנהון [וּמִנְּהֵין] דִּי חֲסַף: לג

³⁴ As you looked on, a stone was hewn out, not by hands, and struck the statue on its feet of iron and clay and crushed them.

חָזֵה הֲוַיְתָ עַד דִּי הִתְגְּזֶרֶת אֶבֶן דִּי־לָא בִידַיִן וּמְחָת לְצַלְמָא עַל־רַגְלוֹהִי דִּי פַרְזְלָא וְחַסְפָּא וְהַדֵּקֶת הִמּוֹן: לד

³⁵ All at once, the iron, clay, bronze, silver, and gold were crushed, and became like chaff of the threshing floors of summer; a wind carried them off until no trace of them was left. But the stone that struck the statue became a great mountain and filled the whole earth.

בֵּאדַיִן דָּקוּ כַחֲדָה פַּרְזְלָא חַסְפָּא נְחָשָׁא כַּסְפָּא וְדַהֲבָא וַהֲווֹ כְּעוּר מִן־אִדְּרֵי־קַיִט וּנְשָׂא הִמּוֹן רוּחָא וְכָל־אֲתַר לָא־הִשְׁתְּכַח לְהוֹן וְאַבְנָא דִּי־מְחָת לְצַלְמָא הֲוָת לְטוּר רַב וּמְלָת כָּל־אַרְעָא: לה

³⁶ "Such was the dream, and we will now tell the king its meaning.

דְּנָה חֶלְמָא וּפִשְׁרֵהּ נֵאמַר קֳדָם־מַלְכָּא: לו

³⁷ You, O king – king of kings, to whom the God of Heaven has given kingdom, power, might, and glory;

אַנְתְּ מַלְכָּא מֶלֶךְ מַלְכַיָּא דִּי אֱלָהּ שְׁמַיָּא מַלְכוּתָא חִסְנָא וְתָקְפָּא וִיקָרָא יְהַב־לָךְ: לז

38 into whose hands He has given men, wild beasts, and the fowl of heaven, wherever they may dwell; and to whom He has given dominion over them all – you are the head of gold.

לח וּבְכָל־דִּי דארין [דָיְרִין] בְּנֵי־אֲנָשָׁא חֵיוַת בָּרָא וְעוֹף־שְׁמַיָּא יְהַב בִּידָךְ וְהַשְׁלְטָךְ בְּכָלְּהוֹן אַנְתְּה־הוּא רֵאשָׁה דִּי דַהֲבָא:

39 But another kingdom will arise after you, inferior to yours; then yet a third kingdom, of bronze, which will rule over the whole earth.

לט וּבָתְרָךְ תְּקוּם מַלְכוּ אָחֳרִי אֲרַע מִנָּךְ וּמַלְכוּ תליתיא [תְלִיתָאָה] אָחֳרִי דִּי נְחָשָׁא דִּי תִשְׁלַט בְּכָל־אַרְעָא:

40 But the fourth kingdom will be as strong as iron; just as iron crushes and shatters everything – and like iron that smashes – so will it crush and smash all these.

מ וּמַלְכוּ רביעיה [רְבִיעָאָה] תֶּהֱוֵא תַקִּיפָה כְּפַרְזְלָא כָּל־קֳבֵל דִּי פַרְזְלָא מְהַדֵּק וְחָשֵׁל כֹּלָּא וּכְפַרְזְלָא דִּי־מְרָעַע כָּל־אִלֵּין תַּדִּק וְתֵרֹעַ:

41 You saw the feet and the toes, part potter's clay and part iron; that means it will be a divided kingdom; it will have only some of the stability of iron, inasmuch as you saw iron mixed with common clay.

מא וְדִי־חֲזַיְתָה רַגְלַיָּא וְאֶצְבְּעָתָא מנהון [מִנְּהֵן] חֲסַף דִּי־פֶחָר וּמִנְּהוֹן [וּמִנְּהֵין] פַּרְזֶל מַלְכוּ פְלִיגָה תֶּהֱוֵה וּמִן־נִצְבְּתָא דִי פַרְזְלָא לֶהֱוֵא־בַהּ כָּל־קֳבֵל דִּי חֲזַיְתָה פַּרְזְלָא מְעָרַב בַּחֲסַף טִינָא:

42 And the toes were part iron and part clay; that [means] the kingdom will be in part strong and in part brittle.

מב וְאֶצְבְּעָת רַגְלַיָּא מִנְּהוֹן [מִנְּהֵין] פַּרְזֶל וּמִנְּהוֹן [וּמִנְּהֵין] חֲסַף מִן־קְצָת מַלְכוּתָא תֶּהֱוֵה תַקִּיפָה וּמִנַּהּ תֶּהֱוֵה תְבִירָה:

43 You saw iron mixed with common clay; that means: they shall intermingle with the offspring of men, but shall not hold together, just as iron does not mix with clay.

מג דִּי [וְדִי] חֲזַיְתָ פַּרְזְלָא מְעָרַב בַּחֲסַף טִינָא מִתְעָרְבִין לֶהֱוֹן בִּזְרַע אֲנָשָׁא וְלָא־לֶהֱוֹן דָּבְקִין דְּנָה עִם־דְּנָה הֵא־כְדִי פַרְזְלָא לָא מִתְעָרַב עִם־חַסְפָּא:

44 And in the time of those kings, the God of Heaven will establish a kingdom that shall never be destroyed, a kingdom that shall not be transferred to another people. It will crush and wipe out all these kingdoms, but shall itself last forever –

מד וּבְיוֹמֵיהוֹן דִּי מַלְכַיָּא אִנּוּן יְקִים אֱלָהּ שְׁמַיָּא מַלְכוּ דִּי לְעָלְמִין לָא תִתְחַבַּל וּמַלְכוּתָה לְעַם אָחֳרָן לָא תִשְׁתְּבִק תַּדִּק וְתָסֵיף כָּל־אִלֵּין מַלְכְוָתָא וְהִיא תְּקוּם לְעָלְמַיָּא:

45 just as you saw how a stone was hewn from the mountain, not by hands, and crushed the iron, bronze, clay, silver, and gold. The great *Hashem* has made known to the king what will happen in the future. The dream is sure and its interpretation reliable."

מה כָּל־קֳבֵל דִּי־חֲזַיְתָ דִּי מִטּוּרָא אִתְגְּזֶרֶת אֶבֶן דִּי־לָא בִידַיִן וְהַדֶּקֶת פַּרְזְלָא נְחָשָׁא חַסְפָּא כַּסְפָּא וְדַהֲבָא אֱלָהּ רַב הוֹדַע לְמַלְכָּא מָה דִּי לֶהֱוֵא אַחֲרֵי דְנָה וְיַצִּיב חֶלְמָא וּמְהֵימַן פִּשְׁרֵהּ:

*kol ko-VAYL dee kha-ZAI-ta DEE mi-tu-RA it-g'-ZE-ret E-ven dee
LA vee-DA-yin v'-ha-DE-ket par-z'-LA n'-kha-SHA khas-PA kas-PA
v'-da-ha-VA e-LAH RAV ho-DA l'-mal-KA MAH DEE le-he-VAY
a-kha-RAY d'-NAH v'-ya-TZEEV khel-MA um-hay-MAN pish-RAY*

2:45 A stone was hewn from the mountain, not by hands Nebuchadnezzar dreams of a statue whose body is comprised of various metals. This dream is a preview of world history. The metals correspond to the four main world powers: The head, made of gold, corresponds to Babylonia, the first kingdom to

46 Then King Nebuchadnezzar prostrated himself and paid homage to *Daniel* and ordered that a meal offering and pleasing offerings be made to him.

מו בֵּאדַ֗יִן מַלְכָּ֤א נְבֽוּכַדְנֶצַּר֙ נְפַ֣ל עַל־אַנְפּ֔וֹהִי וּלְדָנִיֵּ֖אל סְגִ֑ד וּמִנְחָה֙ וְנִ֣יחֹחִ֔ין אֲמַ֖ר לְנַסָּ֥כָה לֵֽהּ׃

47 The king said in reply to *Daniel*, "Truly your God must be the God of gods and Lord of kings and the revealer of mysteries to have enabled you to reveal this mystery."

מז עָנֵה֩ מַלְכָּ֨א לְדָנִיֵּ֜אל וְאָמַ֗ר מִן־קְשֹׁט֙ דִּ֣י אֱלָהֲכ֗וֹן ה֣וּא אֱלָ֤הּ אֱלָהִין֙ וּמָרֵ֣א מַלְכִ֔ין וְגָלֵ֖ה רָזִ֑ין דִּ֣י יְכֵ֔לְתָּ לְמִגְלֵ֖א רָזָ֥ה דְנָֽה׃

48 The king then elevated *Daniel* and gave him very many gifts, and made him governor of the whole province of Babylon and chief prefect of all the wise men of Babylon.

מח אֱדַ֣יִן מַלְכָּ֗א לְדָנִיֵּאל֙ רַבִּ֔י וּמַתְּנָ֤ן רַבְרְבָן֙ שַׂגִּיאָ֣ן יְהַב־לֵ֔הּ וְהַשְׁלְטֵ֗הּ עַ֤ל כָּל־מְדִינַ֣ת בָּבֶ֔ל וְרַ֨ב־סִגְנִ֔ין עַ֖ל כָּל־חַכִּימֵ֥י בָבֶֽל׃

49 At *Daniel*'s request, the king appointed Shadrach, Meshach, and Abednego to administer the province of Babylon; while *Daniel* himself was at the king's court.

מט וְדָנִיֵּאל֙ בְּעָ֣א מִן־מַלְכָּ֔א וּמַנִּ֗י עַ֚ל עֲבִֽידְתָּא֙ דִּ֣י מְדִינַ֣ת בָּבֶ֔ל לְשַׁדְרַ֥ךְ מֵישַׁ֖ךְ וַעֲבֵ֣ד נְג֑וֹ וְדָנִיֵּ֖אל בִּתְרַ֥ע מַלְכָּֽא׃

3 1 King Nebuchadnezzar made a statue of gold sixty *amot* high and six *amot* broad. He set it up in the plain of Dura in the province of Babylon.

ג א נְבוּכַדְנֶצַּ֣ר מַלְכָּ֗א עֲבַד֙ צְלֵ֣ם דִּֽי־דְהַ֔ב רוּמֵהּ֙ אַמִּ֣ין שִׁתִּ֔ין פְּתָיֵ֖הּ אַמִּ֣ין שִׁ֑ת אֲקִימֵהּ֙ בְּבִקְעַ֣ת דּוּרָ֔א בִּמְדִינַ֖ת בָּבֶֽל׃

2 King Nebuchadnezzar then sent word to gather the satraps, prefects, governors, counselors, treasurers, judges, officers, and all the provincial officials to attend the dedication of the statue that King Nebuchadnezzar had set up.

ב וּנְבוּכַדְנֶצַּ֣ר מַלְכָּ֡א שְׁלַ֡ח לְמִכְנַ֣שׁ לַֽאֲחַשְׁדַּרְפְּנַיָּ֡א סִגְנַיָּ֣א וּֽפַחֲוָתָ֡א אֲדַרְגָּזְרַיָּא֩ גְדָ֨בְרַיָּ֤א דְתָֽבְרַיָּא֙ תִּפְתָּיֵ֔א וְכֹ֖ל שִׁלְטֹנֵ֣י מְדִֽינָתָ֑א לְמֵתֵא֙ לַחֲנֻכַּ֣ת צַלְמָ֔א דִּ֥י הֲקֵ֖ים נְבוּכַדְנֶצַּ֥ר מַלְכָּֽא׃

3 So the satraps, prefects, governors, counselors, treasurers, judges, officers, and all the provincial officials assembled for the dedication of the statue that King Nebuchadnezzar had set up, and stood before the statue that Nebuchadnezzar had set up.

ג בֵּאדַ֡יִן מִֽתְכַּנְּשִׁ֡ין אֲחַשְׁדַּרְפְּנַיָּ֡א סִגְנַיָּ֣א וּֽפַחֲוָתָ֡א אֲדַרְגָּזְרַיָּ֣א גְדָֽבְרַיָּ֣א דְּתָֽבְרַיָּ֣א תִּפְתָּיֵ֗א וְכֹל֙ שִׁלְטֹנֵ֣י מְדִֽינָתָ֔א לַחֲנֻכַּ֣ת צַלְמָ֔א דִּ֥י הֲקֵ֖ים נְבוּכַדְנֶצַּ֣ר מַלְכָּ֑א וְקָֽאֲמִ֗ין [וְקָֽיְמִין֙] לָקֳבֵ֣ל צַלְמָ֔א דִּ֥י הֲקֵ֖ים נְבֽוּכַדְנֶצַּֽר׃

4 The herald proclaimed in a loud voice, "You are commanded, O peoples and nations of every language,

ד וְכָרוֹזָ֖א קָרֵ֣א בְחָ֑יִל לְכ֤וֹן אָֽמְרִין֙ עַֽמְמַיָּ֔א אֻמַּיָּ֖א וְלִשָּׁנַיָּֽא׃

The ancient Tower of David in the Old City of *Yerushalayim*

rule the entire known world and defeat the nation of Israel. The chest and arms, fashioned from silver, is symbolic of the Persian-Median empire which defeats the Babylonians. The bronze stomach and thighs represent the Greeks, and the iron legs symbolize the Romans. The clay toes allude to the fact that at the end of the final exile, the Arabs will gain power. As the vision continues, a rock cut from the mountain hits the toes, which symbolizes Israel and the rule of *Mashiach*. According to Rabbi Yitzchak Abrabanel, the rock is cut from the mountain without human intervention, teaching that the final redemption will come about directly from *Hashem*.

Daniel

5 when you hear the sound of the horn, pipe, zither, lyre, psaltery, bagpipe, and all other types of instruments, to fall down and worship the statue of gold that King Nebuchadnezzar has set up.

ה בְּעִדָּנָא דִּי־תִשְׁמְעוּן קָל קַרְנָא מַשְׁרוֹקִיתָא קִיתְרוֹס [קַתְרוֹס] סַבְּכָא פְּסַנְתֵּרִין סוּמְפֹּנְיָה וְכֹל זְנֵי זְמָרָא תִּפְּלוּן וְתִסְגְּדוּן לְצֶלֶם דַּהֲבָא דִּי הֲקֵים נְבוּכַדְנֶצַּר מַלְכָּא:

6 Whoever will not fall down and worship shall at once be thrown into a burning fiery furnace."

ו וּמַן־דִּי־לָא יִפֵּל וְיִסְגֻּד בַּהּ־שַׁעֲתָא יִתְרְמֵא לְגוֹא־אַתּוּן נוּרָא יָקִדְתָּא:

7 And so, as soon as all the peoples heard the sound of the horn, pipe, zither, lyre, psaltery, and all other types of instruments, all peoples and nations of every language fell down and worshiped the statue of gold that King Nebuchadnezzar had set up.

ז כָּל־קֳבֵל דְּנָה בַּהּ־זִמְנָא כְּדִי שָׁמְעִין כָּל־עַמְמַיָּא קָל קַרְנָא מַשְׁרוֹקִיתָא קִיתְרֹס [קַתְרוֹס] שַׂבְּכָא פְּסַנְטֵרִין וְכֹל זְנֵי זְמָרָא נָפְלִין כָּל־עַמְמַיָּא אֻמַיָּא וְלִשָּׁנַיָּא סָגְדִין לְצֶלֶם דַּהֲבָא דִּי הֲקֵים נְבוּכַדְנֶצַּר מַלְכָּא:

8 Seizing the occasion, certain Chaldeans came forward to slander the *Yehudim*.

ח כָּל־קֳבֵל דְּנָה בַּהּ־זִמְנָא קְרִבוּ גֻּבְרִין כַּשְׂדָּאִין וַאֲכַלוּ קַרְצֵיהוֹן דִּי יְהוּדָיֵא:

9 They spoke up and said to King Nebuchadnezzar, "O king, live forever!

ט עֲנוֹ וְאָמְרִין לִנְבוּכַדְנֶצַּר מַלְכָּא מַלְכָּא לְעָלְמִין חֱיִי:

10 You, O king, gave an order that everyone who hears the horn, pipe, zither, lyre, psaltery, bagpipe, and all types of instruments must fall down and worship the golden statue,

י אַנתה [אַנְתְּ] מַלְכָּא שָׂמְתָּ טְּעֵם דִּי כָל־אֱנָשׁ דִּי־יִשְׁמַע קָל קַרְנָא מַשְׁרוֹקִיתָא קִיתְרֹס [קַתְרוֹס] שַׂבְּכָא פְּסַנְתֵּרִין וסיפניה [וְסוּפֹּנְיָה] וְכֹל זְנֵי זְמָרָא יִפֵּל וְיִסְגֻּד לְצֶלֶם דַּהֲבָא:

11 and whoever does not fall down and worship shall be thrown into a burning fiery furnace.

יא וּמַן־דִּי־לָא יִפֵּל וְיִסְגֻּד יִתְרְמֵא לְגוֹא־אַתּוּן נוּרָא יָקִדְתָּא:

12 There are certain *Yehudim* whom you appointed to administer the province of Babylon, Shadrach, Meshach, and Abed-nego; those men pay no heed to you, O king; they do not serve your god or worship the statue of gold that you have set up."

יב אִיתַי גֻּבְרִין יְהוּדָאיִן דִּי־מַנִּיתָ יָתְהוֹן עַל־עֲבִידַת מְדִינַת בָּבֶל שַׁדְרַךְ מֵישַׁךְ וַעֲבֵד נְגוֹ גֻּבְרַיָּא אִלֵּךְ לָא־שָׂמוּ עליך [עֲלָךְ] מַלְכָּא טְעֵם לֵאלָהיך [לֵאלָהָךְ] לָא פָלְחִין וּלְצֶלֶם דַּהֲבָא דִּי הֲקֵימְתָּ לָא סָגְדִין:

13 Then Nebuchadnezzar, in raging fury, ordered Shadrach, Meshach, and Abed-nego to be brought; so those men were brought before the king.

יג בֵּאדַיִן נְבוּכַדְנֶצַּר בִּרְגַז וַחֲמָה אֲמַר לְהַיְתָיָה לְשַׁדְרַךְ מֵישַׁךְ וַעֲבֵד נְגוֹ בֵּאדַיִן גֻּבְרַיָּא אִלֵּךְ הֵיתָיוּ קֳדָם מַלְכָּא:

14 Nebuchadnezzar spoke to them and said, "Is it true, Shadrach, Meshach, and Abed-nego, that you do not serve my god or worship the statue of gold that I have set up?

יד עָנֵה נְבֻכַדְנֶצַּר וְאָמַר לְהוֹן הַצְדָּא שַׁדְרַךְ מֵישַׁךְ וַעֲבֵד נְגוֹ לֵאלָהַי לָא אִיתֵיכוֹן פָּלְחִין וּלְצֶלֶם דַּהֲבָא דִּי הֲקֵימֶת לָא סָגְדִין:

15 Now if you are ready to fall down and worship the statue that I have made when you hear the sound of the horn, pipe, zither, lyre, psaltery, and bagpipe, and all other types of instruments, [well and good]; but if you will not worship, you shall at once

טו כְּעַן הֵן אִיתֵיכוֹן עֲתִידִין דִּי בְעִדָּנָא דִּי־תִשְׁמְעוּן קָל קַרְנָא מַשְׁרוֹקִיתָא קִיתְרֹס [קַתְרוֹס] שַׂבְּכָא פְּסַנְתֵּרִין וְסוּמְפֹּנְיָה וְכֹל זְנֵי זְמָרָא תִּפְּלוּן וְתִסְגְּדוּן לְצַלְמָא דִי־עַבְדֵת וְהֵן לָא תִסְגְּדוּן בַּהּ־שַׁעֲתָה

be thrown into a burning fiery furnace, and what god is there that can save you from my power?"

תִּתְרְמוֹן לְגוֹא־אַתּוּן נוּרָא יָקִדְתָּא וּמַן־הוּא אֱלָהּ דִּי יְשֵׁיזְבִנְכוֹן מִן־יְדָי׃

16 Shadrach, Meshach, and Abed-nego said in reply to the king, "O Nebuchadnezzar, we have no need to answer you in this matter,

טז עֲנוֹ שַׁדְרַךְ מֵישַׁךְ וַעֲבֵד נְגוֹ וְאָמְרִין לְמַלְכָּא נְבוּכַדְנֶצַּר לָא־חַשְׁחִין אֲנַחְנָה עַל־דְּנָה פִּתְגָם לַהֲתָבוּתָךְ׃

17 for if so it must be, our God whom we serve is able to save us from the burning fiery furnace, and He will save us from your power, O king.

יז הֵן אִיתַי אֱלָהַנָא דִּי־אֲנַחְנָא פָלְחִין יָכִל לְשֵׁיזָבוּתַנָא מִן־אַתּוּן נוּרָא יָקִדְתָּא וּמִן־יְדָךְ מַלְכָּא יְשֵׁיזִב׃

18 But even if He does not, be it known to you, O king, that we will not serve your god or worship the statue of gold that you have set up."

יח וְהֵן לָא יְדִיעַ לֶהֱוֵא־לָךְ מַלְכָּא דִּי לֵאלָהָיִךְ [לֵאלָהָךְ] לָא־אִיתַיְנָא [אִיתַנָא] פָלְחִין וּלְצֶלֶם דַּהֲבָא דִּי הֲקֵימְתָּ לָא נִסְגֻּד׃

19 Nebuchadnezzar was so filled with rage at Shadrach, Meshach, and Abed-nego that his visage was distorted, and he gave an order to heat up the furnace to seven times its usual heat.

יט בֵּאדַיִן נְבוּכַדְנֶצַּר הִתְמְלִי חֱמָא וּצְלֵם אַנְפּוֹהִי אֶשְׁתַּנּוּ [אֶשְׁתַּנִּי] עַל־שַׁדְרַךְ מֵישַׁךְ וַעֲבֵד נְגוֹ עָנֵה וְאָמַר לְמֵזֵא לְאַתּוּנָא חַד־שִׁבְעָה עַל דִּי חֲזֵה לְמֵזְיֵהּ׃

20 He commanded some of the strongest men of his army to bind Shadrach, Meshach, and Abed-nego, and to throw them into the burning fiery furnace.

כ וּלְגֻבְרִין גִּבָּרֵי־חַיִל דִּי בְחַיְלֵהּ אֲמַר לְכַפָּתָה לְשַׁדְרַךְ מֵישַׁךְ וַעֲבֵד נְגוֹ לְמִרְמֵא לְאַתּוּן נוּרָא יָקִדְתָּא׃

21 So these men, in their shirts, trousers, hats, and other garments, were bound and thrown into the burning fiery furnace.

כא בֵּאדַיִן גֻּבְרַיָּא אִלֵּךְ כְּפִתוּ בְּסַרְבָּלֵיהוֹן פַּטְּשֵׁיהוֹן [פַּטְּשֵׁיהוֹן] וְכַרְבְּלָתְהוֹן וּלְבֻשֵׁיהוֹן וּרְמִיו לְגוֹא־אַתּוּן נוּרָא יָקִדְתָּא׃

22 Because the king's order was urgent, and the furnace was heated to excess, a tongue of flame killed the men who carried up Shadrach, Meshach, and Abed-nego.

כב כָּל־קֳבֵל דְּנָה מִן־דִּי מִלַּת מַלְכָּא מַחְצְפָה וְאַתּוּנָא אֵזֵה יַתִּירָא גֻּבְרַיָּא אִלֵּךְ דִּי הַסִּקוּ לְשַׁדְרַךְ מֵישַׁךְ וַעֲבֵד נְגוֹ קַטִּל הִמּוֹן שְׁבִיבָא דִּי נוּרָא׃

23 But those three men, Shadrach, Meshach, and Abed-nego, dropped, bound, into the burning fiery furnace.

כג וְגֻבְרַיָּא אִלֵּךְ תְּלָתֵּהוֹן שַׁדְרַךְ מֵישַׁךְ וַעֲבֵד נְגוֹ נְפַלוּ לְגוֹא־אַתּוּן־נוּרָא יָקִדְתָּא מְכַפְּתִין׃

24 Then King Nebuchadnezzar was astonished and, rising in haste, addressed his companions, saying, "Did we not throw three men, bound, into the fire?" They spoke in reply, "Surely, O king."

כד אֱדַיִן נְבוּכַדְנֶצַּר מַלְכָּא תְּוַהּ וְקָם בְּהִתְבְּהָלָה עָנֵה וְאָמַר לְהַדָּבְרוֹהִי הֲלָא גֻבְרִין תְּלָתָא רְמֵינָא לְגוֹא־נוּרָא מְכַפְּתִין עָנַיִן וְאָמְרִין לְמַלְכָּא יַצִּיבָא מַלְכָּא׃

25 He answered, "But I see four men walking about unbound and unharmed in the fire and the fourth looks like a divine being."

כה עָנֵה וְאָמַר הָא־אֲנָה חָזֵה גֻּבְרִין אַרְבְּעָה שְׁרַיִן מַהְלְכִין בְּגוֹא־נוּרָא וַחֲבָל לָא־אִיתַי בְּהוֹן וְרֵוֵהּ דִּי רְבִיעָיָא [רְבִיעָאָה] דָּמֵה לְבַר־אֱלָהִין׃

Daniel

דניאל
פרק ג

26 Nebuchadnezzar then approached the hatch of the burning fiery furnace and called, "Shadrach, Meshach, Abed-nego, servants of the Most High *Hashem*, come out!" So Shadrach, Meshach, and Abed-nego came out of the fire.

כו בֵּאדַ֗יִן קְרֵ֣ב נְבֽוּכַדְנֶצַּ֔ר לִתְרַ֖ע אַתּ֣וּן נוּרָ֣א יָקִֽדְתָּ֑א עָנֵ֣ה וְאָמַ֗ר שַׁדְרַ֤ךְ מֵישַׁךְ֙ וַעֲבֵד־נְגוֹ֙ עַבְד֙וֹהִי֙ דִּֽי־אֱלָהָ֣א עליא [עִלָּאָ֔ה] פֻּ֖קוּ וֶאֱת֑וֹ בֵּאדַ֣יִן נָֽפְקִ֗ין שַׁדְרַ֥ךְ מֵישַׁ֛ךְ וַעֲבֵ֥ד נְג֖וֹ מִן־גּ֥וֹא נוּרָֽא:

27 The satraps, the prefects, the governors, and the royal companions gathered around to look at those men, on whose bodies the fire had had no effect, the hair of whose heads had not been singed, whose shirts looked no different, to whom not even the odor of fire clung.

כז וּ֠מִֽתְכַּנְּשִׁ֠ין אֲחַשְׁדַּרְפְּנַיָּ֨א סִגְנַיָּ֜א וּפַחֲוָתָ֗א וְהַדָּֽבְרֵ֣י מַלְכָּא֮ חָזַ֣יִן לְגֻבְרַיָּ֣א אִלֵּךְ֒ דִּי֩ לָֽא־שְׁלֵ֨ט נוּרָ֜א בְּגֶשְׁמְה֗וֹן וּשְׂעַ֤ר רֵֽאשְׁהוֹן֙ לָ֣א הִתְחָרַ֔ךְ וְסָרְבָּֽלֵיה֖וֹן לָ֣א שְׁנ֑וֹ וְרֵ֣יחַ נ֔וּר לָ֥א עֲדָ֖ת בְּהֽוֹן:

28 Nebuchadnezzar spoke up and said, "Blessed be the God of Shadrach, Meshach, and Abed-nego, who sent His angel to save His servants who, trusting in Him, flouted the king's decree at the risk of their lives rather than serve or worship any god but their own *Hashem*.

כח עָנֵ֨ה נְבֽוּכַדְנֶצַּ֜ר וְאָמַ֗ר בְּרִ֤יךְ אֱלָֽהֲהוֹן֙ דִּֽי־שַׁדְרַ֤ךְ מֵישַׁךְ֙ וַעֲבֵ֣ד נְג֔וֹ דִּֽי־שְׁלַ֤ח מַלְאֲכֵהּ֙ וְשֵׁיזִ֣ב לְעַבְד֔וֹהִי דִּ֥י הִתְרְחִ֖צוּ עֲל֑וֹהִי וּמִלַּ֤ת מַלְכָּא֙ שַׁנִּ֔יו וִיהַ֣בוּ גֶשְׁמְיה֗וֹן [גֶשְׁמְה֗וֹן] דִּ֣י לָֽא־יִפְלְח֤וּן וְלָֽא־יִסְגְּדוּן֙ לְכָל־אֱלָ֔הּ לָהֵ֖ן לֵאלָֽהֲהֽוֹן:

29 I hereby give an order that [anyone of] any people or nation of whatever language who blasphemes the God of Shadrach, Meshach, and Abed-nego shall be torn limb from limb, and his house confiscated, for there is no other God who is able to save in this way."

כט וּמִנִּי֮ שִׂ֣ים טְעֵם֒ דִּי֩ כָל־עַ֨ם אֻמָּ֜ה וְלִשָּׁ֗ן דִּֽי־יֵאמַ֤ר שלה [שָׁלוּ֙] עַ֣ל אֱלָֽהֲה֗וֹן דִּֽי־שַׁדְרַ֤ךְ מֵישַׁךְ֙ וַעֲבֵ֣ד נְג֔וֹא הַדָּמִ֣ין יִתְעֲבֵ֔ד וּבַיְתֵ֖הּ נְוָלִ֣י יִשְׁתַּוֵּ֑ה כָּל־קֳבֵ֗ל דִּ֣י לָ֤א אִיתַ֛י אֱלָ֥הּ אָחֳרָ֖ן דִּֽי־יִכֻּ֥ל לְהַצָּלָ֖ה כִּדְנָֽה:

30 Thereupon the king promoted Shadrach, Meshach, and Abed-nego in the province of Babylon.

ל בֵּאדַ֣יִן מַלְכָּ֗א הַצְלַ֤ח לְשַׁדְרַךְ֙ מֵישַׁ֣ךְ וַעֲבֵ֣ד נְג֔וֹ בִּמְדִינַ֖ת בָּבֶֽל:

*bay-DA-yin mal-KA hatz-LAKH l'-shad-RAKH may-SHAKH
va-a-VAYD n'-GO bim-dee-NAT ba-VEL*

31 "King Nebuchadnezzar to all people and nations of every language that inhabit the whole earth: May your well-being abound!

לא נְבֽוּכַדְנֶצַּ֣ר מַלְכָּ֗א לְֽכָל־עַֽמְמַיָּ֞א אֻמַיָּ֤א וְלִשָּֽׁנַיָּא֙ דִּֽי־דארין [דָיְרִ֣ין] בְּכָל־אַרְעָ֔א שְׁלָמְכ֖וֹן יִשְׂגֵּֽא:

3:30 **The king promoted Shadrach, Meshach, and Abed-nego** These are the Babylonian names of *Chananya*, *Mishael*, and *Azarya*, given to them by the Babylonian chief of officers after they arrived from Israel (1:7). This reference is the last time that *Chananya, Mishael,* and *Azarya* are mentioned in *Sefer Daniel.* One opinion in the Talmud (*Sanhedrin* 83a) suggests that this is because they returned to the Land of Israel. They were motivated practically by their fear of Nebuchadnezzar and what he may do to them next. In addition, they had been elevated spiritually by the miraculous deliverance from the fiery furnace and could no longer tolerate the impuri-

ties of Babylonia. Once in Israel, *Chananya, Mishael,* and *Azarya* learned *Torah* from *Yehoshua* the high priest, married and raised families. This incident contains a message for Jews throughout the ages: When the environment gets hostile in foreign countries, *Eretz Yisrael* provides a safe haven for the Jews. This is true today more than ever, when Jews living outside of Israel still suffer from anti-Semitism. As Prime Minister Golda Meir said about the State of Israel, "Above all, this country is our own. Nobody has to get up in the morning and worry what his neighbors think of him. Being a Jew is no problem here."

Prime Minister
Golda Meir
(1898–1978)

Daniel

10

³² The signs and wonders that the Most High *Hashem* has worked for me I am pleased to relate.

לב אָתַיָּא וְתִמְהַיָּא דִּי עֲבַד עִמִּי אֱלָהָא עליא [עִלָּאָה] שְׁפַר קָדָמַי לְהַחֲוָיָה:

³³ How great are His signs; how mighty His wonders! His kingdom is an everlasting kingdom, and His dominion endures throughout the generations."

לג אָתוֹהִי כְּמָה רַבְרְבִין וְתִמְהוֹהִי כְּמָה תַקִּיפִין מַלְכוּתֵהּ מַלְכוּת עָלַם וְשָׁלְטָנֵהּ עִם־דָּר וְדָר:

4 ¹ I, Nebuchadnezzar, was living serenely in my house, flourishing in my palace.

ד א אֲנָה נְבוּכַדְנֶצַּר שְׁלֵה הֲוֵית בְּבֵיתִי וְרַעְנַן בְּהֵיכְלִי:

² I had a dream that frightened me, and my thoughts in bed and the vision of my mind alarmed me.

ב חֵלֶם חֲזֵית וִידַחֲלִנַּנִי וְהַרְהֹרִין עַל־מִשְׁכְּבִי וְחֶזְוֵי רֵאשִׁי יְבַהֲלֻנַּנִי:

³ I gave an order to bring all the wise men of Babylon before me to let me know the meaning of the dream.

ג וּמִנִּי שִׂים טְעֵם לְהַנְעָלָה קָדָמַי לְכֹל חַכִּימֵי בָבֶל דִּי־פְשַׁר חֶלְמָא יְהוֹדְעֻנַּנִי:

⁴ The magicians, exorcists, Chaldeans, and diviners came, and I related the dream to them, but they could not make its meaning known to me.

ד בֵּאדַיִן עללין [עָלִּין] חַרְטֻמַיָּא אָשְׁפַיָּא כשדיא [כַּשְׂדָּאֵי] וְגָזְרַיָּא וְחֶלְמָא אָמַר אֲנָה קָדָמֵיהוֹן וּפִשְׁרֵהּ לָא־מְהוֹדְעִין לִי:

⁵ Finally, *Daniel*, called Belteshazzar after the name of my god, in whom the spirit of the holy gods was, came to me, and I related the dream to him, [saying],

ה וְעַד אָחֳרֵין עַל קָדָמַי דָּנִיֵּאל דִּי־שְׁמֵהּ בֵּלְטְשַׁאצַּר כְּשֻׁם אֱלָהִי וְדִי רוּחַ־אֱלָהִין קַדִּישִׁין בֵּהּ וְחֶלְמָא קָדָמוֹהִי אַמְרֵת:

⁶ "Belteshazzar, chief magician, in whom I know the spirit of the holy gods to be, and whom no mystery baffles, tell me the meaning of my dream vision that I have seen.

ו בֵּלְטְשַׁאצַּר רַב חַרְטֻמַיָּא דִּי אֲנָה יִדְעֵת דִּי רוּחַ אֱלָהִין קַדִּישִׁין בָּךְ וְכָל־רָז לָא־אָנֵס לָךְ חֶזְוֵי חֶלְמִי דִי־חֲזֵית וּפִשְׁרֵהּ אֱמַר:

⁷ In the visions of my mind in bed I saw a tree of great height in the midst of the earth;

ז וְחֶזְוֵי רֵאשִׁי עַל־מִשְׁכְּבִי חָזֵה הֲוֵית וַאֲלוּ אִילָן בְּגוֹא אַרְעָא וְרוּמֵהּ שַׂגִּיא:

⁸ The tree grew and became mighty; Its top reached heaven, And it was visible to the ends of the earth.

ח רְבָה אִילָנָא וּתְקִף וְרוּמֵהּ יִמְטֵא לִשְׁמַיָּא וַחֲזוֹתֵהּ לְסוֹף כָּל־אַרְעָא:

⁹ Its foliage was beautiful And its fruit abundant; There was food for all in it. Beneath it the beasts of the field found shade, And the birds of the sky dwelt on its branches; All creatures fed on it.

ט עָפְיֵהּ שַׁפִּיר וְאִנְבֵּהּ שַׂגִּיא וּמָזוֹן לְכֹלָּא־בֵהּ תְּחֹתוֹהִי תַּטְלֵל חֵיוַת בָּרָא וּבְעַנְפוֹהִי ידרון [יְדֻרָן] צִפֲּרֵי שְׁמַיָּא וּמִנֵּהּ יִתְּזִין כָּל־בִּשְׂרָא:

¹⁰ In the vision of my mind in bed, I looked and saw a holy Watcher coming down from heaven.

י חָזֵה הֲוֵית בְּחֶזְוֵי רֵאשִׁי עַל־מִשְׁכְּבִי וַאֲלוּ עִיר וְקַדִּישׁ מִן־שְׁמַיָּא נָחִת:

¹¹ He called loudly and said: 'Hew down the tree, lop off its branches, Strip off its foliage, scatter its fruit. Let the beasts of the field flee from beneath it And the birds from its branches,

יא קָרֵא בְחַיִל וְכֵן אָמַר גֹּדּוּ אִילָנָא וְקַצִּצוּ עַנְפוֹהִי אַתַּרוּ עָפְיֵהּ וּבַדַּרוּ אִנְבֵּהּ תְּנֻד חֵיוְתָא מִן־תַּחְתּוֹהִי וְצִפֲּרַיָּא מִן־עַנְפוֹהִי:

¹² But leave the stump with its roots in the ground. In fetters of iron and bronze Let him be drenched with the dew of heaven, And share earth's verdure with the beasts.

יב בְּרַם עִקַּר שָׁרְשׁוֹהִי בְּאַרְעָא שְׁבֻקוּ וּבֶאֱסוּר דִּי־פַרְזֶל וּנְחָשׁ בְּדִתְאָא דִּי בָרָא וּבְטַל שְׁמַיָּא יִצְטַבַּע וְעִם־חֵיוְתָא חֲלָקֵהּ בַּעֲשַׂב אַרְעָא:

13 Let his mind be altered from that of a man, And let him be given the mind of a beast, And let seven seasons pass over him.

יג לִבְבֵהּ מִן־אֲנוֹשָׁא [אֲנָשָׁא] יְשַׁנּוֹן וּלְבַב חֵיוָה יִתְיְהִב לֵהּ וְשִׁבְעָה עִדָּנִין יַחְלְפוּן עֲלוֹהִי:

14 This sentence is decreed by the Watchers; This verdict is commanded by the Holy Ones So that all creatures may know That the Most High is sovereign over the realm of man, And He gives it to whom He wishes And He may set over it even the lowest of men.'

יד בִּגְזֵרַת עִירִין פִּתְגָמָא וּמֵאמַר קַדִּישִׁין שְׁאֵלְתָא עַד־דִּבְרַת דִּי יִנְדְּעוּן חַיַּיָּא דִּי־שַׁלִּיט עִלָּיָא [עִלָּאָה] בְּמַלְכוּת אנושא [אֲנָשָׁא] וּלְמַן־דִּי יִצְבֵּא יִתְּנִנַּהּ וּשְׁפַל אֲנָשִׁים יְקִים עֲליה [עֲלַהּ:]

15 "I, King Nebuchadnezzar, had this dream; now you, Belteshazzar, tell me its meaning, since all the wise men of my kingdom are not able to make its meaning known to me, but you are able, for the spirit of the holy gods is in you."

טו דְּנָה חֶלְמָא חֲזֵית אֲנָה מַלְכָּא נְבוּכַדְנֶצַּר ואנתה [וְאַנְתְּ] בֵּלְטְשַׁאצַּר פִּשְׁרֵא אֱמַר כָּל־קֳבֵל דִּי כָּל־חַכִּימֵי מַלְכוּתִי לָא־ יָכְלִין פִּשְׁרָא לְהוֹדָעֻתַנִי ואנתה [וְאַנְתְּ] כָּהֵל דִּי רוּחַ־אֱלָהִין קַדִּישִׁין בָּךְ:

16 Then *Daniel*, called Belteshazzar, was perplexed for a while, and alarmed by his thoughts. The king addressed him, "Let the dream and its meaning not alarm you." Belteshazzar replied, "My lord, would that the dream were for your enemy and its meaning for your foe!

טז אֱדַיִן דָּנִיֵּאל דִּי־שְׁמֵהּ בֵּלְטְשַׁאצַּר אֶשְׁתּוֹמַם כְּשָׁעָה חֲדָה וְרַעְיֹנֹהִי יְבַהֲלֻנֵּהּ עָנֵה מַלְכָּא וְאָמַר בֵּלְטְשַׁאצַּר חֶלְמָא וּפִשְׁרֵא אַל־יְבַהֲלָךְ עָנֵה בֵלְטְשַׁאצַּר וְאָמַר מראי [מָרִי] חֶלְמָא לְשָׂנְאָיךְ [לְשָׂנְאָךְ] וּפִשְׁרֵהּ לעריך [לְעָרָךְ:]

17 The tree that you saw grow and become mighty, whose top reached heaven, which was visible throughout the earth,

יז אִילָנָא דִּי חֲזַיְתָ דִּי רְבָה וּתְקִף וְרוּמֵהּ יִמְטֵא לִשְׁמַיָּא וַחֲזוֹתֵהּ לְכָל־אַרְעָא:

18 whose foliage was beautiful, whose fruit was so abundant that there was food for all in it, beneath which the beasts of the field dwelt, and in whose branches the birds of the sky lodged –

יח וְעָפְיֵהּ שַׁפִּיר וְאִנְבֵּהּ שַׂגִּיא וּמָזוֹן לְכֹלָּא־ בֵהּ תְּחֹתוֹהִי תְּדוּר חֵיוַת בָּרָא וּבְעַנְפוֹהִי יִשְׁכְּנָן צִפְּרֵי שְׁמַיָּא:

19 it is you, O king, you who have grown and become mighty, whose greatness has grown to reach heaven, and whose dominion is to the end of the earth.

יט אנתה [אַנְתְּ־] הוּא מַלְכָּא דִּי רְבַית וּתְקֵפְתְּ וּרְבוּתָךְ רְבָת וּמְטָת לִשְׁמַיָּא וְשָׁלְטָנָךְ לְסוֹף אַרְעָא:

20 The holy Watcher whom the king saw descend from heaven and say, Hew down the tree and destroy it, But leave the stump with its roots in the ground. In fetters of iron and bronze In the grass of the field, Let him be drenched with the dew of heaven, And share the lot of the beasts of the field Until seven seasons pass over him –

כ וְדִי חֲזָה מַלְכָּא עִיר וְקַדִּישׁ נָחֵת מִן־ שְׁמַיָּא וְאָמַר גֹּדּוּ אִילָנָא וְחַבְּלוּהִי בְּרַם עִקַּר שָׁרְשׁוֹהִי בְּאַרְעָא שְׁבֻקוּ וּבֶאֱסוּר דִּי־פַרְזֶל וּנְחָשׁ בְּדִתְאָא דִּי בָרָא וּבְטַל שְׁמַיָּא יִצְטַבַּע וְעִם־חֵיוַת בָּרָא חֲלָקֵהּ עַד דִּי־שִׁבְעָה עִדָּנִין יַחְלְפוּן עֲלוֹהִי:

21 this is its meaning, O king; it is the decree of the Most High which has overtaken my lord the king.

כא דְּנָה פִשְׁרָא מַלְכָּא וּגְזֵרַת עִלָּיָא [עִלָּאָה] הִיא דִּי מְטָת עַל־מָרִאי [מָרִי] מַלְכָּא:

22 You will be driven away from men and have your habitation with the beasts of the field. You will be fed grass like cattle, and be drenched with the dew of heaven; seven seasons will pass over you until you come to know that the Most High is sovereign over the realm of man, and He gives it to whom He wishes.

כב וְלָךְ טָרְדִין מִן־אֲנָשָׁא וְעִם־חֵיוַת בָּרָא לֶהֱוֵה מְדֹרָךְ וְעִשְׂבָּא כְתוֹרִין לָךְ יְטַעֲמוּן וּמִטַּל שְׁמַיָּא לָךְ מְצַבְּעִין וְשִׁבְעָה עִדָּנִין יַחְלְפוּן עֲלַיִךְ עַד דִּי־תִנְדַּע דִּי־שַׁלִּיט עִלָּיָא בְּמַלְכוּת אֲנָשָׁא וּלְמַן־דִּי יִצְבֵּא יִתְּנִנַּהּ:

23 And the meaning of the command to leave the stump of the tree with its roots is that the kingdom will remain yours from the time you come to know that Heaven is sovereign.

כג וְדִי אֲמַרוּ לְמִשְׁבַּק עִקַּר שָׁרְשׁוֹהִי דִּי אִילָנָא מַלְכוּתָךְ לָךְ קַיָּמָה מִן־דִּי תִנְדַּע דִּי שַׁלִּטִן שְׁמַיָּא:

24 Therefore, O king, may my advice be acceptable to you: Redeem your sins by beneficence and your iniquities by generosity to the poor; then your serenity may be extended."

כד לָהֵן מַלְכָּא מִלְכִּי יִשְׁפַּר עליך [עֲלָךְ] וחטיך [וַחֲטָאָךְ] בְּצִדְקָה פְרֻק וַעֲוָיָתָךְ בְּמִחַן עֲנָיִן הֵן תֶּהֱוֵה אַרְכָה לִשְׁלֵוְתָךְ:

25 All this befell King Nebuchadnezzar.

כה כֹּלָּא מְטָא עַל־נְבוּכַדְנֶצַּר מַלְכָּא:

26 Twelve months later, as he was walking on the roof of the royal palace at Babylon,

כו לִקְצָת יַרְחִין תְּרֵי־עֲשַׂר עַל־הֵיכַל מַלְכוּתָא דִּי בָבֶל מְהַלֵּךְ הֲוָה:

27 the king exclaimed, "There is great Babylon, which I have built by my vast power to be a royal residence for the glory of my majesty!"

כז עָנֵה מַלְכָּא וְאָמַר הֲלָא דָא־הִיא בָּבֶל רַבְּתָא דִּי־אֲנָה בֱנַיְתַהּ לְבֵית מַלְכוּ בִּתְקַף חִסְנִי וְלִיקָר הַדְרִי:

28 The words were still on the king's lips, when a voice fell from heaven, "It has been decreed for you, O King Nebuchadnezzar: The kingdom has passed out of your hands.

כח עוֹד מִלְּתָא בְּפֻם מַלְכָּא קָל מִן־שְׁמַיָּא נְפַל לָךְ אָמְרִין נְבוּכַדְנֶצַּר מַלְכָּא מַלְכוּתָה עֲדָת מִנָּךְ:

29 You are being driven away from men, and your habitation is to be with the beasts of the field. You are to be fed grass like cattle, and seven seasons will pass over you until you come to know that the Most High is sovereign over the realm of man and He gives it to whom He wishes."

כט וּמִן־אֲנָשָׁא לָךְ טָרְדִין וְעִם־חֵיוַת בָּרָא מְדֹרָךְ עִשְׂבָּא כְתוֹרִין לָךְ יְטַעֲמוּן וְשִׁבְעָה עִדָּנִין יַחְלְפוּן עליך [עֲלָךְ] עַד דִּי־תִנְדַּע דִּי־שַׁלִּיט עִלָּיָא בְּמַלְכוּת אֲנָשָׁא וּלְמַן־דִּי יִצְבֵּא יִתְּנִנַּהּ:

u-min a-na-SHA LAKH ta-r'-DEEN v'-eem khay-VAT ba-RA
m'-do-RAKH is-BA kh'-to-REEN LAKH y'-ta-a-MUN v'-shiv-AH
i-da-NEEN yakh-l'-FUN a-LAKH AD dee tin-DA dee sha-LEET i-la-YA
b'-mal-KHUT a-na-SHA ul-man DEE yitz-BAY yit-ni-NAH

4:29 And seven seasons will pass over you In this verse, Nebuchadnezzar is told that he will live with animals and act like a beast for a period of seven seasons. One explanation for this, suggested by the Sages, is that this is a punishment for the way he destroyed *Yerushalayim* and the *Beit Hamikdash*. Although *Hashem* had foretold that the destruction would take place, Nebuchadnezzar did much more than execute God's will. While he was meant to exile the People of Israel, he also killed many of them and treated them inhu-manely. Furthermore, in addition to burning the *Beit Hamikdash*, he also destroyed the earth of *Eretz Yisrael* so that nothing could grow there for seven years. In retribution for his animalistic cruelty to the people and the land, Nebuchadnezzar actually became an animal for seven seasons. His punishment is a lesson about the sensitivity one must show to the People of Israel and the Land of Israel.

A cow grazing on Mount Gilboa

30 There and then the sentence was carried out upon Nebuchadnezzar. He was driven away from men, he ate grass like cattle, and his body was drenched with the dew of heaven until his hair grew like eagle's [feathers] and his nails like [the talons of] birds.

ל בַּהּ־שַׁעֲתָא מִלְּתָא סָפַת עַל־נְבוּכַדְנֶצַּר וּמִן־אֲנָשָׁא טְרִיד וְעִשְׂבָּא כְתוֹרִין יֵאכֻל וּמִטַּל שְׁמַיָּא גִּשְׁמֵהּ יִצְטַבַּע עַד דִּי שַׂעְרֵהּ כְּנִשְׁרִין רְבָה וְטִפְרוֹהִי כְצִפְּרִין:

31 "When the time had passed, I, Nebuchadnezzar, lifted my eyes to heaven, and my reason was restored to me. I blessed the Most High, and praised and glorified the Ever-Living One, Whose dominion is an everlasting dominion And whose kingdom endures throughout the generations.

לא וְלִקְצָת יוֹמַיָּה אֲנָה נְבוּכַדְנֶצַּר עַיְנַי לִשְׁמַיָּא נִטְלֵת וּמַנְדְּעִי עֲלַי יְתוּב וּלְעִלָּאָה [וּלְעִלָּאָה] בָּרְכֵת וּלְחַי עָלְמָא שַׁבְּחֵת וְהַדְּרֵת דִּי שָׁלְטָנֵהּ שָׁלְטָן עָלַם וּמַלְכוּתֵהּ עִם־דָּר וְדָר:

32 All the inhabitants of the earth are of no account. He does as He wishes with the host of heaven, And with the inhabitants of the earth. There is none to stay His hand Or say to Him, 'What have You done?'

לב וְכָל־דָּארֵי [דָּיְרֵי] אַרְעָא כְּלָה חֲשִׁיבִין וּכְמִצְבְּיֵהּ עָבֵד בְּחֵיל שְׁמַיָּא וְדָארֵי [וְדָיְרֵי] אַרְעָא וְלָא אִיתַי דִּי־יְמַחֵא בִידֵהּ וְיֵאמַר לֵהּ מָה עֲבַדְתְּ:

33 There and then my reason was restored to me, and my majesty and splendor were restored to me for the glory of my kingdom. My companions and nobles sought me out, and I was reestablished over my kingdom, and added greatness was given me.

לג בַּהּ־זִמְנָא מַנְדְּעִי יְתוּב עֲלַי וְלִיקַר מַלְכוּתִי הַדְרִי וְזִוִי יְתוּב עֲלַי וְלִי הַדָּבְרַי וְרַבְרְבָנַי יְבַעוֹן וְעַל־מַלְכוּתִי הָתְקְנַת וּרְבוּ יַתִּירָה הוּסְפַת לִי:

34 So now I, Nebuchadnezzar, praise, exalt, and glorify the King of Heaven, all of whose works are just and whose ways are right, and who is able to humble those who behave arrogantly."

לד כְּעַן אֲנָה נְבוּכַדְנֶצַּר מְשַׁבַּח וּמְרוֹמֵם וּמְהַדַּר לְמֶלֶךְ שְׁמַיָּא דִּי כָל־מַעֲבָדוֹהִי קְשֹׁט וְאֹרְחָתֵהּ דִּין וְדִי מַהְלְכִין בְּגֵוָה יָכִל לְהַשְׁפָּלָה:

5 1 King Belshazzar gave a great banquet for his thousand nobles, and in the presence of the thousand he drank wine.

ה א בֵּלְשַׁאצַּר מַלְכָּא עֲבַד לְחֶם רַב לְרַבְרְבָנוֹהִי אֲלַף וְלָקֳבֵל אַלְפָּא חַמְרָא שָׁתֵה:

bayl-sha-TZAR mal-KA a-vad l'-KHEM RAV l'-rav-r'-va-NO-hee a-LAF v'-la-ko-VAYL al-PA kham-RA sha-TAY

Daniel

5:1 King Belshazzar gave a great banquet Years before, *Yirmiyahu* issued his famous prophecy that Babylonia would rule over the Jews for seventy years (Jeremiah 29:10). *Malbim* comments that according to Belshazzar's calculations, these seventy years have now elapsed and he is still in power. He therefore throws a feast to mark this milestone, and uses the holy vessels from the *Beit Hamikdash* in *Yerushalayim* to further illustrate this point (verse 2). *Hashem* responds with the famous writing that appears on the wall during the feast, and by morning, Belshazzar is dead. Rabbi Yitzchak Abrabanel adds that this incident plants much hope in the hearts of the People of Israel, who realize that God can turn events around in an instant. He coordinates everything and is precise in His calculations. The Jews of *Daniel*'s time witness that those who mistreat them will ultimately pay for their actions.

Model of the second *Beit Hamikdash* in *Yerushalayim*

2 Under the influence of the wine, Belshazzar ordered the gold and silver vessels that his father Nebuchadnezzar had taken out of the temple at *Yerushalayim* to be brought so that the king and his nobles, his consorts, and his concubines could drink from them.

ב בֵּלְשַׁאצַּר אֲמַר בִּטְעֵם חַמְרָא לְהַיְתָיָה לְמָאנֵי דַּהֲבָא וְכַסְפָּא דִּי הַנְפֵּק נְבוּכַדְנֶצַּר אֲבוּהִי מִן־הֵיכְלָא דִּי בִירוּשְׁלֶם וְיִשְׁתּוֹן בְּהוֹן מַלְכָּא וְרַבְרְבָנוֹהִי שֵׁגְלָתֵהּ וּלְחֵנָתֵהּ:

3 The golden vessels that had been taken out of the sanctuary of the House of *Hashem* in *Yerushalayim* were then brought, and the king, his nobles, his consorts, and his concubines drank from them.

ג בֵּאדַיִן הַיְתִיו מָאנֵי דַהֲבָא דִּי הַנְפִּקוּ מִן־הֵיכְלָא דִי־בֵית אֱלָהָא דִּי בִירוּשְׁלֶם וְאִשְׁתִּיו בְּהוֹן מַלְכָּא וְרַבְרְבָנוֹהִי שֵׁגְלָתֵהּ וּלְחֵנָתֵהּ:

4 They drank wine and praised the gods of gold and silver, bronze, iron, wood, and stone.

ד אִשְׁתִּיו חַמְרָא וְשַׁבַּחוּ לֵאלָהֵי דַּהֲבָא וְכַסְפָּא נְחָשָׁא פַרְזְלָא אָעָא וְאַבְנָא:

5 Just then, the fingers of a human hand appeared and wrote on the plaster of the wall of the king's palace opposite the lampstand, so that the king could see the hand as it wrote.

ה בַּהּ־שַׁעֲתָה נְפַקוּ [נְפַקָה] אֶצְבְּעָן דִּי יַד־אֱנָשׁ וְכָתְבָן לָקֳבֵל נֶבְרַשְׁתָּא עַל־גִּירָא דִּי־כְתַל הֵיכְלָא דִּי מַלְכָּא וּמַלְכָּא חָזֵה פַּס יְדָה דִּי כָתְבָה:

6 The king's face darkened, and his thoughts alarmed him; the joints of his loins were loosened and his knees knocked together.

ו אֱדַיִן מַלְכָּא זִיוֹהִי שְׁנוֹהִי וְרַעְיֹנֹהִי יְבַהֲלוּנֵּהּ וְקִטְרֵי חַרְצֵהּ מִשְׁתָּרַיִן וְאַרְכֻבָּתֵהּ דָּא לְדָא נָקְשָׁן:

7 The king called loudly for the exorcists, Chaldeans, and diviners to be brought. The king addressed the wise men of Babylon, "Whoever can read this writing and tell me its meaning shall be clothed in purple and wear a golden chain on his neck, and shall rule as one of three in the kingdom."

ז קָרֵא מַלְכָּא בְּחַיִל לְהֶעָלָה לְאָשְׁפַיָּא כשדיא [כַּשְׂדָּאֵי] וְגָזְרַיָּא עָנֵה מַלְכָּא וְאָמַר לְחַכִּימֵי בָבֶל דִּי כָל־אֱנָשׁ דִּי־יִקְרֵה כְּתָבָה דְנָה וּפִשְׁרֵהּ יְחַוִּנַּנִי אַרְגְּוָנָא יִלְבַּשׁ והמונכא [וְהַמְנִיכָא] דִי־דַהֲבָא עַל־צַוְּארֵהּ וְתַלְתִּי בְמַלְכוּתָא יִשְׁלַט:

8 Then all the king's wise men came, but they could not read the writing or make known its meaning to the king.

ח אֱדַיִן עללין [עָלִּין] כֹּל חַכִּימֵי מַלְכָּא וְלָא־כָהֲלִין כְּתָבָא לְמִקְרֵא ופשרה [וּפִשְׁרֵהּ] לְהוֹדָעָה לְמַלְכָּא:

9 King Belshazzar grew exceedingly alarmed and his face darkened, and his nobles were dismayed.

ט אֱדַיִן מַלְכָּא בֵלְשַׁאצַּר שַׂגִּיא מִתְבָּהַל וְזִיוֹהִי שָׁנַיִן עֲלוֹהִי וְרַבְרְבָנוֹהִי מִשְׁתַּבְּשִׁין:

10 Because of the state of the king and his nobles, the queen came to the banquet hall. The queen spoke up and said, "O king, live forever! Let your thoughts not alarm you or your face darken.

י מַלְכְּתָא לָקֳבֵל מִלֵּי מַלְכָּא וְרַבְרְבָנוֹהִי לְבֵית מִשְׁתְּיָא עללת [עַלַּת] עֲנָת מַלְכְּתָא וַאֲמֶרֶת מַלְכָּא לְעָלְמִין חֱיִי אַל־יְבַהֲלוּךְ רַעְיוֹנָךְ וְזִיוָיךְ אַל־יִשְׁתַּנּוֹ:

11 There is a man in your kingdom who has the spirit of the holy gods in him; in your father's time, illumination, understanding, and wisdom like that of the gods were to be found in him, and your father, King Nebuchadnezzar, appointed him chief of the magicians, exorcists, Chaldeans, and diviners.

יא אִיתַי גְּבַר בְּמַלְכוּתָךְ דִּי רוּחַ אֱלָהִין קַדִּישִׁין בֵּהּ וּבְיוֹמֵי אֲבוּךְ נַהִירוּ וְשָׂכְלְתָנוּ וְחָכְמָה כְּחָכְמַת־אֱלָהִין הִשְׁתְּכַחַת בֵּהּ וּמַלְכָּא נְבֻכַדְנֶצַּר אֲבוּךְ רַב חַרְטֻמִּין אָשְׁפִין כַּשְׂדָּאִין גָּזְרִין הֲקִימֵהּ אֲבוּךְ מַלְכָּא:

12 Seeing that there is to be found in *Daniel* (whom the king called Belteshazzar) extraordinary spirit, knowledge, and understanding to interpret dreams, to explain riddles and solve problems, let *Daniel* now be called to tell the meaning [of the writing]."

יב כָּל־קֳבֵל דִּי רוּחַ יַתִּירָה וּמַנְדַּע וְשָׂכְלְתָנוּ מְפַשַּׁר חֶלְמִין וַאַחֲוָיַת אֲחִידָן וּמְשָׁרֵא קִטְרִין הִשְׁתְּכַחַת בֵּהּ בְּדָנִיֵּאל דִּי־מַלְכָּא שָׂם־שְׁמֵהּ בֵּלְטְשַׁאצַּר כְּעַן דָּנִיֵּאל יִתְקְרֵי וּפִשְׁרָה יְהַחֲוֵה:

13 *Daniel* was then brought before the king. The king addressed *Daniel*, "You are *Daniel*, one of the exiles of *Yehuda* whom my father, the king, brought from *Yehuda*.

יג בֵּאדַיִן דָּנִיֵּאל הֻעַל קֳדָם מַלְכָּא עָנֵה מַלְכָּא וְאָמַר לְדָנִיֵּאל אנתה־[אַנְתְּ] הוּא דָנִיֵּאל דִּי־מִן־בְּנֵי גָלוּתָא דִּי יְהוּד דִּי הַיְתִי מַלְכָּא אַבִי מִן־יְהוּד:

14 I have heard about you that you have the spirit of the gods in you, and that illumination, knowledge, and extraordinary wisdom are to be found in you.

יד וְשִׁמְעֵת עליך [עֲלָךְ] דִּי רוּחַ אֱלָהִין בָּךְ וְנַהִירוּ וְשָׂכְלְתָנוּ וְחָכְמָה יַתִּירָה הִשְׁתְּכַחַת בָּךְ:

15 Now the wise men and exorcists have been brought before me to read this writing and to make known its meaning to me. But they could not tell what it meant.

טו וּכְעַן הֻעַלּוּ קָדָמַי חַכִּימַיָּא אָשְׁפַיָּא דִּי־כְתָבָה דְנָה יִקְרוֹן וּפִשְׁרֵהּ לְהוֹדָעֻתַנִי וְלָא־כָהֲלִין פְּשַׁר־מִלְּתָא לְהַחֲוָיָה:

16 I have heard about you, that you can give interpretations and solve problems. Now if you can read the writing and make known its meaning to me, you shall be clothed in purple and wear a golden chain on your neck and rule as one of three in the kingdom."

טז וַאֲנָה שִׁמְעֵת עליך [עֲלָךְ] דִּי־תוכל [תִיכוּל] פִּשְׁרִין לְמִפְשַׁר וְקִטְרִין לְמִשְׁרֵא כְּעַן הֵן תוכל [תִּכוּל] כְּתָבָא לְמִקְרֵא וּפִשְׁרֵהּ לְהוֹדָעֻתַנִי אַרְגְּוָנָא תִלְבַּשׁ והמונכא [וְהַמְנִיכָא] דִי־דַהֲבָא עַל־צַוְּארָךְ וְתַלְתָּא בְמַלְכוּתָא תִּשְׁלַט:

17 Then *Daniel* said in reply to the king, "You may keep your gifts for yourself, and give your presents to others. But I will read the writing for the king, and make its meaning known to him.

יז בֵּאדַיִן עָנֵה דָנִיֵּאל וְאָמַר קֳדָם מַלְכָּא מַתְּנָתָךְ לָךְ לֶהֶוְיָן וּנְבָזְבְּיָתָךְ לְאָחֳרָן הַב בְּרַם כְּתָבָא אֶקְרֵא לְמַלְכָּא וּפִשְׁרָא אֲהוֹדְעִנֵּהּ:

18 O king, the Most High *Hashem* bestowed kingship, grandeur, glory, and majesty upon your father Nebuchadnezzar.

יח אנתה [אַנְתְּ] מַלְכָּא אֱלָהָא עליא [עִלָּאָה] מַלְכוּתָא וּרְבוּתָא וִיקָרָא וְהַדְרָה יְהַב לִנְבֻכַדְנֶצַּר אֲבוּךְ:

19 And because of the grandeur that He bestowed upon him, all the peoples and nations of every language trembled in fear of him. He put to death whom he wished, and whom he wished he let live; he raised high whom he wished and whom he wished he brought low.

יט וּמִן־רְבוּתָא דִּי יְהַב־לֵהּ כֹּל עַמְמַיָּא אֻמַיָּא וְלִשָּׁנַיָּא הֲווֹ זאעין [זָיְעִין] וְדָחֲלִין מִן־קֳדָמוֹהִי דִּי־הֲוָה צָבֵא הֲוָא קָטֵל וְדִי־הֲוָה צָבֵא הֲוָה מַחֵא וְדִי־הֲוָה צָבֵא הֲוָה מָרִים וְדִי־הֲוָה צָבֵא הֲוָה מַשְׁפִּיל:

20 But when he grew haughty and willfully presumptuous, he was deposed from his royal throne and his glory was removed from him.

כ וּכְדִי רִם לִבְבֵהּ וְרוּחֵהּ תִּקְפַת לַהֲזָדָה הָנְחַת מִן־כָּרְסֵא מַלְכוּתֵהּ וִיקָרָה הֶעְדִּיו מִנֵּהּ:

21 He was driven away from men, and his mind made like that of a beast, and his habitation was with wild asses. He was fed grass like cattle, and his body was drenched with the dew of heaven until he came to know that the Most High *Hashem* is sovereign over the realm of man, and sets over it whom He wishes.

כא וּמִן־בְּנֵי אֲנָשָׁא טְרִיד וְלִבְבֵהּ עִם־חֵיוְתָא שוי [שַׁוִּיו] וְעִם־עֲרָדַיָּא מְדוֹרֵהּ עִשְׂבָּא כְתוֹרִין יְטַעֲמוּנֵּהּ וּמִטַּל שְׁמַיָּא גִּשְׁמֵהּ יִצְטַבַּע עַד דִּי־יְדַע דִּי־שַׁלִּיט אֱלָהָא עליא [עִלָּאָה] בְּמַלְכוּת אֲנָשָׁא וּלְמַן־דִּי יִצְבֵּה יְהָקֵים עליה [עֲלַהּ]:

22 But you, Belshazzar his son, did not humble yourself although you knew all this.

כב וְאַנְתְּ [וְאַנְתָּ] בְּרֵהּ בֵּלְשַׁאצַּר לָא הַשְׁפֵּלְתְּ לִבְבָךְ כָּל־קֳבֵל דִּי כָל־דְּנָה יְדַעְתָּ׃

23 You exalted yourself against the Lord of Heaven, and had the vessels of His temple brought to you. You and your nobles, your consorts, and your concubines drank wine from them and praised the gods of silver and gold, bronze and iron, wood and stone, which do not see, hear, or understand; but the God who controls your lifebreath and every move you make – Him you did not glorify!

כג וְעַל מָרֵא־שְׁמַיָּא הִתְרוֹמַמְתָּ וּלְמָאנַיָּא דִי־בַיְתֵהּ הַיְתִיו קדמיך [קָדָמָךְ] ואנתה [וְאַנְתְּ] ורברבניך [וְרַבְרְבָנָךְ] שֵׁגְלָתָךְ וּלְחֵנָתָךְ חַמְרָא שָׁתַיִן בְּהוֹן וְלֵאלָהֵי כַסְפָּא־וְדַהֲבָא נְחָשָׁא פַרְזְלָא אָעָא וְאַבְנָא דִּי לָא־חָזַיִן וְלָא־שָׁמְעִין וְלָא יָדְעִין שַׁבַּחְתָּ וְלֵאלָהָא דִּי־נִשְׁמְתָךְ בִּידֵהּ וְכָל־אֹרְחָתָךְ לֵהּ לָא הַדַּרְתָּ׃

24 He therefore made the hand appear, and caused the writing to be inscribed.

כד בֵּאדַיִן מִן־קֳדָמוֹהִי שְׁלִיַח פַּסָּא דִי־יְדָא וּכְתָבָא דְנָה רְשִׁים׃

25 This is the writing that is inscribed: mene mene tekel upharsin.

כה וּדְנָה כְתָבָא דִּי רְשִׁים מְנֵא מְנֵא תְּקֵל וּפַרְסִין׃

26 And this is its meaning: mene – *Hashem* has numbered [the days of] your kingdom and brought it to an end;

כו דְּנָה פְּשַׁר־מִלְּתָא מְנֵא מְנָה־אֱלָהָא מַלְכוּתָךְ וְהַשְׁלְמַהּ׃

27 tekel – you have been weighed in the balance and found wanting;

כז תְּקֵל תְּקִילְתָּה בְמֹאזַנְיָא וְהִשְׁתְּכַחַתְּ חַסִּיר׃

28 peres – your kingdom has been divided and given to the Medes and the Persians."

כח פְּרֵס פְּרִיסַת מַלְכוּתָךְ וִיהִיבַת לְמָדַי וּפָרָס׃

29 Then, at Belshazzar's command, they clothed *Daniel* in purple, placed a golden chain on his neck, and proclaimed that he should rule as one of three in the kingdom.

כט בֵּאדַיִן אֲמַר בֵּלְשַׁאצַּר וְהַלְבִּישׁו לְדָנִיֵּאל אַרְגְּוָנָא והמונכא [וְהַמְנִיכָא] דִי־דַהֲבָא עַל־צַוְּארֵהּ וְהַכְרִזוּ עֲלוֹהִי דִּי־לֶהֱוֵא שַׁלִּיט תַּלְתָּא בְּמַלְכוּתָא׃

30 That very night, Belshazzar, the Chaldean king, was killed,

ל בֵּהּ בְּלֵילְיָא קְטִיל בֵּלְאשַׁצַּר מַלְכָּא כשדיא [כַשְׂדָּאָה]׃

6 ¹ and Darius the Mede received the kingdom, being about sixty-two years old.

א וְדָרְיָוֶשׁ מָדָיָא קַבֵּל מַלְכוּתָא כְּבַר שְׁנִין שִׁתִּין וְתַרְתֵּין׃

2 It pleased Darius to appoint over the kingdom one hundred and twenty satraps to be in charge of the whole kingdom;

ב שְׁפַר קֳדָם דָּרְיָוֶשׁ וַהֲקִים עַל־מַלְכוּתָא לַאֲחַשְׁדַּרְפְּנַיָּא מְאָה וְעֶשְׂרִין דִּי לֶהֱוֹן בְּכָל־מַלְכוּתָא׃

3 over them were three ministers, one of them *Daniel*, to whom these satraps reported, in order that the king not be troubled.

ג וְעֵלָּא מִנְּהוֹן סָרְכִין תְּלָתָא דִּי דָנִיֵּאל חַד־מִנְּהוֹן דִּי־לֶהֱוֹן אֲחַשְׁדַּרְפְּנַיָּא אִלֵּין יָהֲבִין לְהוֹן טַעְמָא וּמַלְכָּא לָא־לֶהֱוֵא נָזִק׃

4 This man *Daniel* surpassed the other ministers and satraps by virtue of his extraordinary spirit, and the king considered setting him over the whole kingdom.

ד אֱדַיִן דָּנִיֵּאל דְּנָה הֲוָא מִתְנַצַּח עַל־סָרְכַיָּא וַאֲחַשְׁדַּרְפְּנַיָּא כָּל־קֳבֵל דִּי רוּחַ יַתִּירָא בֵּהּ וּמַלְכָּא עֲשִׁית לַהֲקָמוּתֵהּ עַל־כָּל־מַלְכוּתָא׃

5 The ministers and satraps looked for some fault in *Daniel*'s conduct in matters of state, but they could find neither fault nor corruption, inasmuch as he was trustworthy, and no negligence or corruption was to be found in him.

ה אֱדַיִן סָרְכַיָּא וַאֲחַשְׁדַּרְפְּנַיָּא הֲווֹ בָעַיִן עִלָּה לְהַשְׁכָּחָה לְדָנִיֵּאל מִצַּד מַלְכוּתָא וְכָל־עִלָּה וּשְׁחִיתָה לָא־יָכְלִין לְהַשְׁכָּחָה כָּל־קֳבֵל דִּי־מְהֵימַן הוּא וְכָל־שָׁלוּ וּשְׁחִיתָה לָא הִשְׁתְּכַחַת עֲלוֹהִי:

6 Those men then said, "We are not going to find any fault with this *Daniel*, unless we find something against him in connection with the laws of his God."

ו אֱדַיִן גֻּבְרַיָּא אִלֵּךְ אָמְרִין דִּי לָא נְהַשְׁכַּח לְדָנִיֵּאל דְּנָה כָּל־עִלָּא לָהֵן הַשְׁכַּחְנָה עֲלוֹהִי בְּדָת אֱלָהֵהּ:

7 Then these ministers and satraps came thronging in to the king and said to him, "O King Darius, live forever!

ז אֱדַיִן סָרְכַיָּא וַאֲחַשְׁדַּרְפְּנַיָּא אִלֵּן הַרְגִּשׁוּ עַל־מַלְכָּא וְכֵן אָמְרִין לֵהּ דָּרְיָוֶשׁ מַלְכָּא לְעָלְמִין חֱיִי:

8 All the ministers of the kingdom, the prefects, satraps, companions, and governors are in agreement that a royal ban should be issued under sanction of an oath that whoever shall address a petition to any god or man, besides you, O king, during the next thirty days shall be thrown into a lions' den.

ח אִתְיָעַטוּ כֹּל סָרְכֵי מַלְכוּתָא סִגְנַיָּא וַאֲחַשְׁדַּרְפְּנַיָּא הַדָּבְרַיָּא וּפַחֲוָתָא לְקַיָּמָה קְיָם מַלְכָּא וּלְתַקָּפָה אֱסָר דִּי כָל־דִּי־יִבְעֵה בָעוּ מִן־כָּל־אֱלָהּ וֶאֱנָשׁ עַד־יוֹמִין תְּלָתִין לָהֵן מִנָּךְ מַלְכָּא יִתְרְמֵא לְגֹב אַרְיָוָתָא:

9 So issue the ban, O king, and put it in writing so that it be unalterable as a law of the Medes and Persians that may not be abrogated."

ט כְּעַן מַלְכָּא תְּקִים אֱסָרָא וְתִרְשֻׁם כְּתָבָא דִּי לָא לְהַשְׁנָיָה כְּדָת־מָדַי וּפָרַס דִּי־לָא תֶעְדֵּא:

10 Thereupon King Darius put the ban in writing.

י כָּל־קֳבֵל דְּנָה מַלְכָּא דָּרְיָוֶשׁ רְשַׁם כְּתָבָא וֶאֱסָרָא:

11 When *Daniel* learned that it had been put in writing, he went to his house, in whose upper chamber he had had windows made facing *Yerushalayim*, and three times a day he knelt down, prayed, and made confession to his God, as he had always done.

יא וְדָנִיֵּאל כְּדִי יְדַע דִּי־רְשִׁים כְּתָבָא עַל לְבַיְתֵהּ וְכַוִּין פְּתִיחָן לֵהּ בְּעִלִּיתֵהּ נֶגֶד יְרוּשְׁלֶם וְזִמְנִין תְּלָתָה בְיוֹמָא הוּא בָּרֵךְ עַל־בִּרְכוֹהִי וּמְצַלֵּא וּמוֹדֵא קֳדָם אֱלָהֵהּ כָּל־קֳבֵל דִּי־הֲוָא עָבֵד מִן־קַדְמַת דְּנָה:

v'-da-ni-YAYL k'-DEE y'-DA dee r'-SHEEM k'-ta-VA AL l'-vai-TAY v'-kha-VEEN p'-tee-KHAN LAY b'-i-lee-TAY NE-ged y'-ru-sh'-LEM v'-zim-NEEN t'-la-TA v'-yo-MA HU ba-RAYKH al bir-KHO-hee um-tza-LAY u-mo-DAY ko-DAM e-la-HAY kol ko-VAYL dee ha-VA a-VAYD min kad-MAT d'-NAH

6:11 He had windows made facing *Yerushalayim*
Even though *Hashem*'s Temple had been destroyed for fifty years, *Daniel* continues to turn in its direction when praying. Indeed, Jews throughout the ages have maintained the tradition of praying facing *Yerushalayim*, showing their eternal connection with their holy city. This is a fulfillment of King *Shlomo*'s wish when dedicating the *Beit Hamikdash* (I Kings 8:48–49): "They turn back to You with all their heart and soul, in the land of the enemies… and they pray to You in the direction of their land which You gave to their fathers, of the city which You have chosen, and of the House which I have built to Your name – oh, give heed in Your heavenly abode to their prayer and supplication…" The deep bond between the Jewish people and the city of Jerusalem can be found throughout *Tanakh*.

Praying at the Western Wall in *Yerushalayim*

18

12 Then those men came thronging in and found *Daniel* petitioning his God in supplication.

יב אֱדַ֣יִן גֻּבְרַיָּ֤א אִלֵּךְ֙ הַרְגִּ֔שׁוּ וְהַשְׁכַּ֖חוּ לְדָנִיֵּ֑אל בָּעֵ֥א וּמִתְחַנַּ֖ן קֳדָ֥ם אֱלָהֵֽהּ׃

13 They then approached the king and reminded him of the royal ban: "Did you not put in writing a ban that whoever addresses a petition to any god or man besides you, O king, during the next thirty days, shall be thrown into a lions' den?" The king said in reply, "The order stands firm, as a law of the Medes and Persians that may not be abrogated."

יג בֵּאדַ֜יִן קְרִ֣יבוּ וְאָמְרִ֣ין קֳדָם־מַלְכָּ֘א עַל־אֱסָ֣ר מַלְכָּ֒א הֲלָ֧א אֱסָ֣ר רְשַׁ֗מְתָּ דִּ֣י כָל־אֱנָ֡שׁ דִּֽי־יִבְעֵה֩ מִן־כָּל־אֱלָ֨הּ וֶֽאֱנָ֜שׁ עַד־יוֹמִ֣ין תְּלָתִ֗ין לָהֵן֙ מִנָּ֣ךְ מַלְכָּ֔א יִתְרְמֵ֕א לְג֖וֹב אַרְיָוָתָ֑א עָנֵ֨ה מַלְכָּ֜א וְאָמַ֗ר יַצִּיבָ֤ה מִלְּתָא֙ כְּדָת־מָדַ֣י וּפָרַ֔ס דִּי־לָ֖א תֶעְדֵּֽא׃

14 Thereupon they said to the king, "*Daniel*, one of the exiles of *Yehuda*, pays no heed to you, O king, or to the ban that you put in writing; three times a day he offers his petitions [to his God]."

יד בֵּאדַ֜יִן עֲנ֣וֹ וְאָמְרִין֮ קֳדָ֣ם מַלְכָּא֒ דִּ֣י דָנִיֵּ֡אל דִּי֩ מִן־בְּנֵ֨י גָלוּתָ֜א דִּ֣י יְה֗וּד לָֽא־שָׂ֨ם עֲלַ֤יִךְ [עֲלָךְ֙] מַלְכָּ֣א טְעֵ֔ם וְעַ֨ל־אֱסָרָ֖א דִּ֣י רְשַׁ֑מְתָּ וְזִמְנִ֤ין תְּלָתָה֙ בְּיוֹמָ֔א בָּעֵ֖א בָּעוּתֵֽהּ׃

15 Upon hearing that, the king was very disturbed, and he set his heart upon saving *Daniel*, and until the sun set made every effort to rescue him.

טו אֱדַ֨יִן מַלְכָּ֜א כְּדִ֧י מִלְּתָ֣א שְׁמַ֗ע שַׂגִּיא֙ בְּאֵ֣שׁ עֲל֔וֹהִי וְעַ֧ל דָּנִיֵּ֛אל שָׂ֥ם בָּ֖ל לְשֵׁיזָבוּתֵ֑הּ וְעַד֙ מֶֽעָלֵ֣י שִׁמְשָׁ֔א הֲוָ֥א מִשְׁתַּדַּ֖ר לְהַצָּלוּתֵֽהּ׃

16 Then those men came thronging in to the king and said to the king, "Know, O king, that it is a law of the Medes and Persians that any ban that the king issues under sanction of oath is unalterable."

טז בֵּאדַ֙יִן֙ גֻּבְרַיָּ֣א אִלֵּ֔ךְ הַרְגִּ֖שׁוּ עַל־מַלְכָּ֑א וְאָמְרִ֣ין לְמַלְכָּ֗א דַּ֤ע מַלְכָּא֙ דִּֽי־דָ֣ת לְמָדַ֣י וּפָרַ֔ס דִּֽי־כָל־אֱסָ֥ר וּקְיָ֛ם דִּֽי־מַלְכָּ֥א יְהָקֵ֖ים לָ֥א לְהַשְׁנָיָֽה׃

17 By the king's order, *Daniel* was then brought and thrown into the lions' den. The king spoke to *Daniel* and said, "Your God, whom you serve so regularly, will deliver you."

יז בֵּאדַ֤יִן מַלְכָּא֙ אֲמַ֔ר וְהַיְתִ֙יו֙ לְדָ֣נִיֵּ֔אל וּרְמ֕וֹ לְגֻבָּ֖א דִּ֣י אַרְיָוָתָ֑א עָנֵ֤ה מַלְכָּא֙ וְאָמַ֣ר לְדָנִיֵּ֔אל אֱלָהָ֗ךְ דִּ֣י אַ֙נתה [אַ֙נתְּ֙] פָּֽלַֽח־לֵהּ֙ בִּתְדִירָ֔א ה֖וּא יְשֵׁיזְבִנָּֽךְ׃

18 A rock was brought and placed over the mouth of the den; the king sealed it with his signet and with the signet of his nobles, so that nothing might be altered concerning *Daniel*.

יח וְהֵיתָ֙יִת֙ אֶ֣בֶן חֲדָ֔ה וְשֻׂמַ֖ת עַל־פֻּ֣ם גֻּבָּ֑א וְחַתְמַ֨הּ מַלְכָּ֜א בְּעִזְקְתֵ֗הּ וּבְעִזְקָת֙ רַבְרְבָנ֔וֹהִי דִּ֛י לָא־תִשְׁנֵ֥א צְב֖וּ בְּדָנִיֵּֽאל׃

19 The king then went to his palace and spent the night fasting; no diversions were brought to him, and his sleep fled from him.

יט אֱדַ֜יִן אֲזַ֤ל מַלְכָּא֙ לְהֵ֣יכְלֵ֔הּ וּבָ֖ת טְוָ֑ת וְדַחֲוָ֖ן לָא־הַנְעֵ֣ל קָֽדָמ֑וֹהִי וְשִׁנְתֵּ֖הּ נַדַּ֥ת עֲלֽוֹהִי׃

20 Then, at the first light of dawn, the king arose and rushed to the lions' den.

כ בֵּאדַ֣יִן מַלְכָּ֗א בִּשְׁפַּרְפָּרָא֙ יְק֣וּם בְּנָגְהָ֔א וּבְהִ֨תְבְּהָלָ֔ה לְגֻבָּ֥א דִֽי־אַרְיָוָתָ֖א אֲזַֽל׃

21 As he approached the den, he cried to *Daniel* in a mournful voice; the king said to *Daniel*, "*Daniel*, servant of the living *Hashem*, was the God whom you served so regularly able to deliver you from the lions?"

כא וּכְמִקְרְבֵ֣הּ לְגֻבָּ֔א לְדָ֣נִיֵּ֔אל בְּקָ֥ל עֲצִ֖יב זְעִ֑ק עָנֵ֨ה מַלְכָּ֜א וְאָמַ֣ר לְדָנִיֵּ֗אל דָּֽנִיֵּאל֙ עֲבֵד֙ אֱלָהָ֣א חַיָּ֔א אֱלָהָ֗ךְ דִּ֣י אַ֙נתה [אַ֙נתְּ֙] פָּֽלַֽח־לֵהּ֙ בִּתְדִירָ֔א הַיְכִ֥ל לְשֵׁיזָבוּתָ֖ךְ מִן־אַרְיָוָתָֽא׃

22 *Daniel* then talked with the king, "O king, live forever!

כב אֱדַ֙יִן֙ דָּנִיֵּ֔אל עִם־מַלְכָּ֖א מַלִּ֑ל מַלְכָּ֖א לְעָלְמִ֥ין חֱיִֽי׃

23 My *Hashem* sent His angel, who shut the mouths of the lions so that they did not injure me, inasmuch as I was found innocent by Him, nor have I, O king, done you any injury."

כג אֱלָהִי שְׁלַח מַלְאֲכֵהּ וּסֲגַר פֻּם אַרְיָוָתָא וְלָא חַבְּלוּנִי כָּל־קֳבֵל דִּי קֳדָמוֹהִי זָכוּ הִשְׁתְּכַחַת לִי וְאַף קדמיך [קָֽדָמָךְ] מַלְכָּא חֲבוּלָה לָא עַבְדֵֽת:

24 The king was very glad, and ordered *Daniel* to be brought up out of the den. *Daniel* was brought up out of the den, and no injury was found on him, for he had trusted in his God.

כד בֵּאדַיִן מַלְכָּא שַׂגִּיא טְאֵֽב עֲלוֹהִי וּלְדָנִיֵּאל אֲמַר לְהַנְסָקָה מִן־גֻּבָּא וְהֻסַּק דָּנִיֵּאל מִן־גֻּבָּא וְכָל־חֲבָל לָא־הִשְׁתְּכַח בֵּהּ דִּי הֵימִן בֵּאלָהֵֽהּ:

25 Then, by order of the king, those men who had slandered *Daniel* were brought and, together with their children and wives, were thrown into the lions' den. They had hardly reached the bottom of the den when the lions overpowered them and crushed all their bones.

כה וַאֲמַר מַלְכָּא וְהַיְתִיו גֻּבְרַיָּא אִלֵּךְ דִּֽי־אֲכַלוּ קַרְצוֹהִי דִּי דָנִיֵּאל וּלְגֹב אַרְיָוָתָא רְמוֹ אִנּוּן בְּנֵיהוֹן וּנְשֵׁיהוֹן וְלָא־מְטוֹ לְאַרְעִית גֻּבָּא עַד דִּֽי־שְׁלִטֽוּ בְהוֹן אַרְיָוָתָא וְכָל־גַּרְמֵיהוֹן הַדִּֽקוּ:

26 Then King Darius wrote to all peoples and nations of every language that inhabit the earth, "May your well-being abound!

כו בֵּאדַיִן דָּֽרְיָוֶשׁ מַלְכָּא כְּתַב לְכָל־עַֽמְמַיָּא אֻמַּיָּא וְלִשָּׁנַיָּא דִּֽי־דארין [דָֽיְרִין] בְּכָל־אַרְעָא שְׁלָמְכוֹן יִשְׂגֵּֽא:

27 I have hereby given an order that throughout my royal domain men must tremble in fear before the God of *Daniel*, for He is the living *Hashem* who endures forever; His kingdom is indestructible, and His dominion is to the end of time;

כז מִן־קֳדָמַי שִׂים טְעֵם דִּי בְּכָל־שָׁלְטָן מַלְכוּתִי לֶהֱוֺן זאעין [זָיְעִין] וְדָֽחֲלִין מִן־קֳדָם אֱלָהֵהּ דִּֽי־דָֽנִיֵּאל דִּי־הוּא אֱלָהָא חַיָּא וְקַיָּם לְעָלְמִין וּמַלְכוּתֵהּ דִּֽי־לָא תִתְחַבַּל וְשָׁלְטָנֵהּ עַד־סוֹפָֽא:

28 He delivers and saves, and performs signs and wonders in heaven and on earth, for He delivered *Daniel* from the power of the lions."

כח מְשֵׁיזִב וּמַצִּל וְעָבֵד אָתִין וְתִמְהִין בִּשְׁמַיָּא וּבְאַרְעָא דִּי שֵׁיזִיב לְדָנִיֵּאל מִן־יַד אַרְיָוָתָֽא:

29 Thus *Daniel* prospered during the reign of Darius and during the reign of Cyrus the Persian.

כט וְדָנִיֵּאל דְּנָה הַצְלַח בְּמַלְכוּת דָּֽרְיָוֶשׁ וּבְמַלְכוּת כּוֹרֶשׁ פרסיא [פָּרְסָאָֽה]:

7 1 In the first year of King Belshazzar of Babylon, *Daniel* saw a dream and a vision of his mind in bed; afterward he wrote down the dream. Beginning the account,

ז א בִּשְׁנַת חֲדָה לְבֵלְאשַׁצַּר מֶלֶךְ בָּבֶל דָּנִיֵּאל חֵלֶם חֲזָה וְחֶזְוֵי רֵאשֵׁהּ עַל־מִשְׁכְּבֵהּ בֵּאדַיִן חֶלְמָא כְתַב רֵאשׁ מִלִּין אֲמַֽר:

bish-NAT kha-DAH l'-vayl-sha-TZAR ME-lekh ba-VEL da-ni-YAYL
KHAY-lem kha-ZAH v'-khez-VAY ray-SHAY al mish-k'-VAY
bay-DA-yin khel-MA kh'-TAV RAYSH mi-LEEN a-MAR

Daniel

7:1 *Daniel* saw a dream Lest anyone think that history is coincidental, *Hashem* shows *Daniel* a preview of all that will transpire until the end of days. According to Rabbi Yitzchak Abrabanel, *Daniel's* visions are meant to comfort the Jewish people throughout their long and bitter exile. *Hashem* is like a doctor who explains a difficult treatment to his patient, but promises that all the painful symptoms guarantee a full recovery at the end. When we see that the predicted suffering has occurred, we can be assured that redemption, with all the promise it holds, will come true as well. For 2000 years history has been witness to much Jewish suffering. Finally, with the establishment of the State of Israel in 1948, the process of recovery has begun.

David Ben Gurion declaring the State of Israel, 1948

2 *Daniel* related the following: "In my vision at night, I saw the four winds of heaven stirring up the great sea.

ב עָנֵה דָנִיֵּאל וְאָמַר חָזֵה הֲוֵית בְּחֶזְוִי עִם־לֵילְיָא וַאֲרוּ אַרְבַּע רוּחֵי שְׁמַיָּא מְגִיחָן לְיַמָּא רַבָּא:

3 Four mighty beasts different from each other emerged from the sea.

ג וְאַרְבַּע חֵיוָן רַבְרְבָן סָלְקָן מִן־יַמָּא שָׁנְיָן דָּא מִן־דָּא:

4 The first was like a lion but had eagles' wings. As I looked on, its wings were plucked off, and it was lifted off the ground and set on its feet like a man and given the mind of a man.

ד קַדְמָיְתָא כְאַרְיֵה וְגַפִּין דִּי־נְשַׁר לַהּ חָזֵה הֲוֵית עַד דִּי־מְּרִיטוּ גַפַּיהּ וּנְטִילַת מִן־אַרְעָא וְעַל־רַגְלַיִן כֶּאֱנָשׁ הֳקִימַת וּלְבַב אֱנָשׁ יְהִיב לַהּ:

5 Then I saw a second, different beast, which was like a bear but raised on one side, and with three fangs in its mouth among its teeth; it was told, 'Arise, eat much meat!'

ה וַאֲרוּ חֵיוָה אָחֳרִי תִנְיָנָה דָּמְיָה לְדֹב וְלִשְׂטַר־חַד הֳקִמַת וּתְלָת עִלְעִין בְּפֻמַּהּ בֵּין שִׁנַּיהּ [שִׁנַּהּ] וְכֵן אָמְרִין לַהּ קוּמִי אֲכֻלִי בְּשַׂר שַׂגִּיא:

6 After that, as I looked on, there was another one, like a leopard, and it had on its back four wings like those of a bird; the beast had four heads, and dominion was given to it.

ו בָּאתַר דְּנָה חָזֵה הֲוֵית וַאֲרוּ אָחֳרִי כִּנְמַר וְלַהּ גַּפִּין אַרְבַּע דִּי־עוֹף עַל־גַּבַּיַּהּ [גַּבַּהּ] וְאַרְבְּעָה רֵאשִׁין לְחֵיוְתָא וְשָׁלְטָן יְהִיב לַהּ:

7 After that, as I looked on in the night vision, there was a fourth beast – fearsome, dreadful, and very powerful, with great iron teeth – that devoured and crushed, and stamped the remains with its feet. It was different from all the other beasts which had gone before it; and it had ten horns.

ז בָּאתַר דְּנָה חָזֵה הֲוֵית בְּחֶזְוֵי לֵילְיָא וַאֲרוּ חֵיוָה רְבִיעָיה [רְבִיעָאָה] דְּחִילָה וְאֵימְתָנִי וְתַקִּיפָא יַתִּירָא וְשִׁנַּיִן דִּי־פַרְזֶל לַהּ רַבְרְבָן אָכְלָה וּמַדֱּקָה וּשְׁאָרָא בְּרַגְלַיהּ [בְּרַגְלַהּ] רָפְסָה וְהִיא מְשַׁנְּיָה מִן־כָּל־חֵיוָתָא דִּי קָדָמַיהּ וְקַרְנַיִן עֲשַׂר לַהּ:

8 While I was gazing upon these horns, a new little horn sprouted up among them; three of the older horns were uprooted to make room for it. There were eyes in this horn like those of a man, and a mouth that spoke arrogantly.

ח מִשְׂתַּכַּל הֲוֵית בְּקַרְנַיָּא וַאֲלוּ קֶרֶן אָחֳרִי זְעֵירָה סִלְקָת בֵּינֵיהוֹן [בֵּינֵיהֵן] וּתְלָת מִן־קַרְנַיָּא קַדְמָיָתָא אֶתְעֲקַרוּ [אֶתְעֲקַרָה] מִן־קֳדָמַיהּ [קֳדָמַהּ] וַאֲלוּ עַיְנִין כְּעַיְנֵי אֲנָשָׁא בְּקַרְנָא־דָא וּפֻם מְמַלִּל רַבְרְבָן:

9 As I looked on, Thrones were set in place, And the Ancient of Days took His seat. His garment was like white snow, And the hair of His head was like lamb's wool. His throne was tongues of flame; Its wheels were blazing fire.

ט חָזֵה הֲוֵית עַד דִּי כָרְסָוָן רְמִיו וְעַתִּיק יוֹמִין יְתִב לְבוּשֵׁהּ כִּתְלַג חִוָּר וּשְׂעַר רֵאשֵׁהּ כַּעֲמַר נְקֵא כָּרְסְיֵהּ שְׁבִיבִין דִּי־נוּר גַּלְגִּלּוֹהִי נוּר דָּלִק:

10 A river of fire streamed forth before Him; Thousands upon thousands served Him; Myriads upon myriads attended Him; The court sat and the books were opened.

י נְהַר דִּי־נוּר נָגֵד וְנָפֵק מִן־קֳדָמוֹהִי אֶלֶף אלפים [אַלְפִין] יְשַׁמְּשׁוּנֵּהּ וְרִבּוֹ רבון [רִבְבָן] קָדָמוֹהִי יְקוּמוּן דִּינָא יְתִב וְסִפְרִין פְּתִיחוּ:

11 I looked on. Then, because of the arrogant words that the horn spoke, the beast was killed as I looked on; its body was destroyed and it was consigned to the flames.

יא חָזֵה הֲוֵית בֵּאדַיִן מִן־קָל מִלַּיָּא רַבְרְבָתָא דִּי קַרְנָא מְמַלֱּלָה חָזֵה הֲוֵית עַד דִּי קְטִילַת חֵיוְתָא וְהוּבַד גִּשְׁמַהּ וִיהִיבַת לִיקֵדַת אֶשָּׁא:

12 The dominion of the other beasts was taken away, but an extension of life was given to them for a time and season.

יב וּשְׁאָר חֵיוָתָא הֶעְדִּיו שָׁלְטָנְהוֹן וְאַרְכָה בְחַיִּין יְהִיבַת לְהוֹן עַד־זְמַן וְעִדָּן:

13 As I looked on, in the night vision, One like a human being Came with the clouds of heaven; He reached the Ancient of Days And was presented to Him.

יג חָזֵה הֲוֵית בְּחֶזְוֵי לֵילְיָא וַאֲרוּ עִם־עֲנָנֵי שְׁמַיָּא כְּבַר אֱנָשׁ אָתֵה הֲוָה וְעַד־עַתִּיק יוֹמַיָּא מְטָה וּקְדָמוֹהִי הַקְרְבוּהִי:

14 Dominion, glory, and kingship were given to him; All peoples and nations of every language must serve him. His dominion is an everlasting dominion that shall not pass away, And his kingship, one that shall not be destroyed.

יד וְלֵהּ יְהִיב שָׁלְטָן וִיקָר וּמַלְכוּ וְכֹל עַמְמַיָּא אֻמַיָּא וְלִשָּׁנַיָּא לֵהּ יִפְלְחוּן שָׁלְטָנֵהּ שָׁלְטָן עָלַם דִּי־לָא יֶעְדֵּה וּמַלְכוּתֵהּ דִּי־לָא תִתְחַבַּל:

15 As for me, *Daniel*, my spirit was disturbed within me and the vision of my mind alarmed me.

טו אֶתְכְּרִיַּת רוּחִי אֲנָה דָנִיֵּאל בְּגוֹא נִדְנֶה וְחֶזְוֵי רֵאשִׁי יְבַהֲלֻנַּנִי:

16 I approached one of the attendants and asked him the true meaning of all this. He gave me this interpretation of the matter:

טז קִרְבֵת עַל־חַד מִן־קָאֲמַיָּא וְיַצִּיבָא אֶבְעֵא־מִנֵּהּ עַל־כָּל־דְּנָה וַאֲמַר־לִי וּפְשַׁר מִלַּיָּא יְהוֹדְעִנַּנִי:

17 'These great beasts, four in number [mean] four kingdoms will arise out of the earth;

יז אִלֵּין חֵיוָתָא רַבְרְבָתָא דִּי אִנִּין אַרְבַּע אַרְבְּעָה מַלְכִין יְקוּמוּן מִן־אַרְעָא:

18 then holy ones of the Most High will receive the kingdom, and will possess the kingdom forever – forever and ever.'

יח וִיקַבְּלוּן מַלְכוּתָא קַדִּישֵׁי עֶלְיוֹנִין וְיַחְסְנוּן מַלְכוּתָא עַד־עָלְמָא וְעַד עָלַם עָלְמַיָּא:

19 Then I wanted to ascertain the true meaning of the fourth beast, which was different from them all, very fearsome, with teeth of iron, claws of bronze, that devoured and crushed, and stamped the remains;

יט אֱדַיִן צְבִית לְיַצָּבָא עַל־חֵיוְתָא רְבִיעָיְתָא דִּי־הֲוָת שָׁנְיָה מִן־כָּלְּהוֹן [כָּלְהֵין] דְּחִילָה יַתִּירָה שניה [שִׁנַּהּ] דִּי־פַרְזֶל וְטִפְרַיהּ דִּי־נְחָשׁ אָכְלָה מַדֲּקָה וּשְׁאָרָא בְּרַגְלַיהּ רָפְסָה:

20 and of the ten horns on its head; and of the new one that sprouted, to make room for which three fell – the horn that had eyes, and a mouth that spoke arrogantly, and which was more conspicuous than its fellows.

כ וְעַל־קַרְנַיָּא עֲשַׂר דִּי בְרֵאשַׁהּ וְאָחֳרִי דִּי סִלְקַת וּנְפַלוּ [וּנְפַלָה] מִן־קֳדָמַיהּ [קֳדָמַהּ] תְּלָת וְקַרְנָא דִכֵּן וְעַיְנִין לַהּ וְפֻם מְמַלִּל רַבְרְבָן וְחֶזְוַהּ רַב מִן־חַבְרָתַהּ:

21 (I looked on as that horn made war with the holy ones and overcame them,

כא חָזֵה הֲוֵית וְקַרְנָא דִכֵּן עָבְדָה קְרָב עִם־קַדִּישִׁין וְיָכְלָה לְהוֹן:

22 until the Ancient of Days came and judgment was rendered in favor of the holy ones of the Most High, for the time had come, and the holy ones took possession of the kingdom.)

כב עַד דִּי־אֲתָה עַתִּיק יוֹמַיָּא וְדִינָא יְהִב לְקַדִּישֵׁי עֶלְיוֹנִין וְזִמְנָא מְטָה וּמַלְכוּתָא הֶחֱסִנוּ קַדִּישִׁין:

23 This is what he said: 'The fourth beast [means] – there will be a fourth kingdom upon the earth which will be different from all the kingdoms; it will devour the whole earth, tread it down, and crush it.

כג כֵּן אֲמַר חֵיוְתָא רְבִיעָיְתָא מַלְכוּ רביעיא [רְבִיעָאָה] תֶּהֱוֵא בְאַרְעָא דִּי תִשְׁנֵא מִן־כָּל־מַלְכְוָתָא וְתֵאכֻל כָּל־אַרְעָא וּתְדוּשִׁנַּהּ וְתַדְּקִנַּהּ:

24 And the ten horns [mean] – from that kingdom, ten kings will arise, and after them another will arise. He will be different from the former ones, and will bring low three kings.

כד וְקַרְנַיָּא עֲשַׂר מִנַּהּ מַלְכוּתָה עַשְׂרָה מַלְכִין יְקֻמוּן וְאָחֳרָן יְקוּם אַחֲרֵיהוֹן וְהוּא יִשְׁנֵא מִן־קַדְמָיֵא וּתְלָתָה מַלְכִין יְהַשְׁפִּל:

25 He will speak words against the Most High, and will harass the holy ones of the Most High. He will think of changing times and laws, and they will be delivered into his power for a time, times, and half a time.

כה וּמִלִּין לְצַד עליא [עִלָּאָה] יְמַלִּל וּלְקַדִּישֵׁי עֶלְיוֹנִין יְבַלֵּא וְיִסְבַּר לְהַשְׁנָיָה זִמְנִין וְדָת וְיִתְיַהֲבוּן בִּידֵהּ עַד־עִדָּן וְעִדָּנִין וּפְלַג עִדָּן:

26 Then the court will sit and his dominion will be taken away, to be destroyed and abolished for all time.

כו וְדִינָא יִתִּב וְשָׁלְטָנֵהּ יְהַעְדּוֹן לְהַשְׁמָדָה וּלְהוֹבָדָה עַד־סוֹפָא:

27 The kingship and dominion and grandeur belonging to all the kingdoms under Heaven will be given to the people of the holy ones of the Most High. Their kingdom shall be an everlasting kingdom, and all dominions shall serve and obey them.'"

כז וּמַלְכוּתָה וְשָׁלְטָנָא וּרְבוּתָא דִּי מַלְכְוָת תְּחוֹת כָּל־שְׁמַיָּא יְהִיבַת לְעַם קַדִּישֵׁי עֶלְיוֹנִין מַלְכוּתֵהּ מַלְכוּת עָלַם וְכֹל שָׁלְטָנַיָּא לֵהּ יִפְלְחוּן וְיִשְׁתַּמְּעוּן:

28 Here the account ends. I, *Daniel*, was very alarmed by my thoughts, and my face darkened; and I could not put the matter out of my mind.

כח עַד־כָּה סוֹפָא דִי־מִלְּתָא אֲנָה דָנִיֵּאל שַׂגִּיא רַעְיוֹנַי יְבַהֲלֻנַּנִי וְזִיוַי יִשְׁתַּנּוֹן עֲלַי וּמִלְּתָא בְּלִבִּי נִטְרֵת:

8 ¹ In the third year of the reign of King Belshazzar, a vision appeared to me, to me, *Daniel*, after the one that had appeared to me earlier.

ח א בִּשְׁנַת שָׁלוֹשׁ לְמַלְכוּת בֵּלְאשַׁצַּר הַמֶּלֶךְ חָזוֹן נִרְאָה אֵלַי אֲנִי דָנִיֵּאל אַחֲרֵי הַנִּרְאָה אֵלַי בַּתְּחִלָּה:

2 I saw in the vision – at the time I saw it I was in the fortress of Shushan, in the province of Elam – I saw in the vision that I was beside the Ulai River.

ב וָאֶרְאֶה בֶּחָזוֹן וַיְהִי בִּרְאֹתִי וַאֲנִי בְּשׁוּשַׁן הַבִּירָה אֲשֶׁר בְּעֵילָם הַמְּדִינָה וָאֶרְאֶה בֶּחָזוֹן וַאֲנִי הָיִיתִי עַל־אוּבַל אוּלָי:

3 I looked and saw a ram standing between me and the river; he had two horns; the horns were high, with one higher than the other, and the higher sprouting last.

ג וָאֶשָּׂא עֵינַי וָאֶרְאֶה וְהִנֵּה אַיִל אֶחָד עֹמֵד לִפְנֵי הָאֻבָל וְלוֹ קְרָנַיִם וְהַקְּרָנַיִם גְּבֹהוֹת וְהָאַחַת גְּבֹהָה מִן־הַשֵּׁנִית וְהַגְּבֹהָה עֹלָה בָּאַחֲרֹנָה:

4 I saw the ram butting westward, northward, and southward. No beast could withstand him, and there was none to deliver from his power. He did as he pleased and grew great.

ד רָאִיתִי אֶת־הָאַיִל מְנַגֵּחַ יָמָּה וְצָפוֹנָה וָנֶגְבָּה וְכָל־חַיּוֹת לֹא־יַעַמְדוּ לְפָנָיו וְאֵין מַצִּיל מִיָּדוֹ וְעָשָׂה כִרְצֹנוֹ וְהִגְדִּיל:

5 As I looked on, a he-goat came from the west, passing over the entire earth without touching the ground. The goat had a conspicuous horn on its forehead.

ה וַאֲנִי הָיִיתִי מֵבִין וְהִנֵּה צְפִיר־הָעִזִּים בָּא מִן־הַמַּעֲרָב עַל־פְּנֵי כָל־הָאָרֶץ וְאֵין נוֹגֵעַ בָּאָרֶץ וְהַצָּפִיר קֶרֶן חָזוּת בֵּין עֵינָיו:

6 He came up to the two-horned ram that I had seen standing between me and the river and charged at him with furious force.

ו וַיָּבֹא עַד־הָאַיִל בַּעַל הַקְּרָנַיִם אֲשֶׁר רָאִיתִי עֹמֵד לִפְנֵי הָאֻבָל וַיָּרָץ אֵלָיו בַּחֲמַת כֹּחוֹ:

Daniel

7 I saw him reach the ram and rage at him; he struck the ram and broke its two horns, and the ram was powerless to withstand him. He threw him to the ground and trampled him, and there was none to deliver the ram from his power.

ז וּרְאִיתִיו מַגִּיעַ אֵצֶל הָאַיִל וַיִּתְמַרְמַר אֵלָיו וַיַּךְ אֶת־הָאַיִל וַיְשַׁבֵּר אֶת־שְׁתֵּי קְרָנָיו וְלֹא־הָיָה כֹחַ בָּאַיִל לַעֲמֹד לְפָנָיו וַיַּשְׁלִיכֵהוּ אַרְצָה וַיִּרְמְסֵהוּ וְלֹא־הָיָה מַצִּיל לָאַיִל מִיָּדוֹ:

8 Then the he-goat grew very great, but at the peak of his power his big horn was broken. In its place, four conspicuous horns sprouted toward the four winds of heaven.

ח וּצְפִיר הָעִזִּים הִגְדִּיל עַד־מְאֹד וּכְעָצְמוֹ נִשְׁבְּרָה הַקֶּרֶן הַגְּדוֹלָה וַתַּעֲלֶנָה חָזוּת אַרְבַּע תַּחְתֶּיהָ לְאַרְבַּע רוּחוֹת הַשָּׁמָיִם:

9 From one of them emerged a small horn, which extended itself greatly toward the south, toward the east, and toward the beautiful land.

ט וּמִן־הָאַחַת מֵהֶם יָצָא קֶרֶן־אַחַת מִצְּעִירָה וַתִּגְדַּל־יֶתֶר אֶל־הַנֶּגֶב וְאֶל־הַמִּזְרָח וְאֶל־הַצֶּבִי:

10 It grew as high as the host of heaven and it hurled some stars of the [heavenly] host to the ground and trampled them.

י וַתִּגְדַּל עַד־צְבָא הַשָּׁמָיִם וַתַּפֵּל אַרְצָה מִן־הַצָּבָא וּמִן־הַכּוֹכָבִים וַתִּרְמְסֵם:

11 It vaunted itself against the very chief of the host; on its account the regular offering was suspended, and His holy place was abandoned.

יא וְעַד שַׂר־הַצָּבָא הִגְדִּיל וּמִמֶּנּוּ הרים [הוּרַם] הַתָּמִיד וְהֻשְׁלַךְ מְכוֹן מִקְדָּשׁוֹ:

12 An army was arrayed iniquitously against the regular offering; it hurled truth to the ground and prospered in what it did.

יב וְצָבָא תִּנָּתֵן עַל־הַתָּמִיד בְּפָשַׁע וְתַשְׁלֵךְ אֱמֶת אַרְצָה וְעָשְׂתָה וְהִצְלִיחָה:

13 Then I heard a holy being speaking, and another holy being said to whoever it was who was speaking, "How long will [what was seen in] the vision last – the regular offering be forsaken because of transgression; the sanctuary be surrendered and the [heavenly] host be trampled?"

יג וָאֶשְׁמְעָה אֶחָד־קָדוֹשׁ מְדַבֵּר וַיֹּאמֶר אֶחָד קָדוֹשׁ לַפַּלְמוֹנִי הַמְדַבֵּר עַד־מָתַי הֶחָזוֹן הַתָּמִיד וְהַפֶּשַׁע שֹׁמֵם תֵּת וְקֹדֶשׁ וְצָבָא מִרְמָס:

14 He answered me, "For twenty-three hundred evenings and mornings; then the sanctuary shall be cleansed."

יד וַיֹּאמֶר אֵלַי עַד עֶרֶב בֹּקֶר אַלְפַּיִם וּשְׁלֹשׁ מֵאוֹת וְנִצְדַּק קֹדֶשׁ:

15 While I, Daniel, was seeing the vision, and trying to understand it, there appeared before me one who looked like a man.

טו וַיְהִי בִּרְאֹתִי אֲנִי דָנִיֵּאל אֶת־הֶחָזוֹן וָאֲבַקְשָׁה בִינָה וְהִנֵּה עֹמֵד לְנֶגְדִּי כְּמַרְאֵה־גָבֶר:

16 I heard a human voice from the middle of Ulai calling out, "Gabriel, make that man understand the vision."

טז וָאֶשְׁמַע קוֹל־אָדָם בֵּין אוּלָי וַיִּקְרָא וַיֹּאמַר גַּבְרִיאֵל הָבֵן לְהַלָּז אֶת־הַמַּרְאֶה:

17 He came near to where I was standing, and as he came I was terrified, and fell prostrate. He said to me, "Understand, O man, that the vision refers to the time of the end."

יז וַיָּבֹא אֵצֶל עָמְדִי וּבְבֹאוֹ נִבְעַתִּי וָאֶפְּלָה עַל־פָּנָי וַיֹּאמֶר אֵלַי הָבֵן בֶּן־אָדָם כִּי לְעֶת־קֵץ הֶחָזוֹן:

18 When he spoke with me, I was overcome by a deep sleep as I lay prostrate on the ground. Then he touched me and made me stand up,

יח וּבְדַבְּרוֹ עִמִּי נִרְדַּמְתִּי עַל־פָּנַי אָרְצָה וַיִּגַּע־בִּי וַיַּעֲמִידֵנִי עַל־עָמְדִי:

19 and said, "I am going to inform you of what will happen when wrath is at an end, for [it refers] to the time appointed for the end.

יט וַיֹּאמֶר הִנְנִי מוֹדִיעֲךָ אֵת אֲשֶׁר־יִהְיֶה בְּאַחֲרִית הַזָּעַם כִּי לְמוֹעֵד קֵץ׃

20 "The two-horned ram that you saw [signifies] the kings of Media and Persia;

כ הָאַיִל אֲשֶׁר־רָאִיתָ בַּעַל הַקְּרָנָיִם מַלְכֵי מָדַי וּפָרָס׃

21 and the buck, the he-goat – the king of Greece; and the large horn on his forehead, that is the first king.

כא וְהַצָּפִיר הַשָּׂעִיר מֶלֶךְ יָוָן וְהַקֶּרֶן הַגְּדוֹלָה אֲשֶׁר בֵּין־עֵינָיו הוּא הַמֶּלֶךְ הָרִאשׁוֹן׃

v'-ha-tza-FEER ha-sa-EER ME-lekh ya-VAN v'-ha-KE-ren ha-g'-do-LAH a-SHER BAYN ay-NAV hu ha-ME-lekh ha-ri-SHON

22 One was broken and four came in its stead – that [means]: four kingdoms will arise out of a nation, but without its power.

כב וְהַנִּשְׁבֶּרֶת וַתַּעֲמֹדְנָה אַרְבַּע תַּחְתֶּיהָ אַרְבַּע מַלְכֻיּוֹת מִגּוֹי יַעֲמֹדְנָה וְלֹא בְכֹחוֹ׃

23 When their kingdoms are at an end, when the measure of transgression has been filled, then a king will arise, impudent and versed in intrigue.

כג וּבְאַחֲרִית מַלְכוּתָם כְּהָתֵם הַפֹּשְׁעִים יַעֲמֹד מֶלֶךְ עַז־פָּנִים וּמֵבִין חִידוֹת׃

24 He will have great strength, but not through his own strength. He will be extraordinarily destructive; he will prosper in what he does, and destroy the mighty and the people of holy ones.

כד וְעָצַם כֹּחוֹ וְלֹא בְכֹחוֹ וְנִפְלָאוֹת יַשְׁחִית וְהִצְלִיחַ וְעָשָׂה וְהִשְׁחִית עֲצוּמִים וְעַם־קְדֹשִׁים׃

25 By his cunning, he will use deceit successfully. He will make great plans, will destroy many, taking them unawares, and will rise up against the chief of chiefs, but will be broken, not by [human] hands.

כה וְעַל־שִׂכְלוֹ וְהִצְלִיחַ מִרְמָה בְּיָדוֹ וּבִלְבָבוֹ יַגְדִּיל וּבְשַׁלְוָה יַשְׁחִית רַבִּים וְעַל־שַׂר־שָׂרִים יַעֲמֹד וּבְאֶפֶס יָד יִשָּׁבֵר׃

26 What was said in the vision about evenings and mornings is true. Now you keep the vision a secret, for it pertains to far-off days."

כו וּמַרְאֵה הָעֶרֶב וְהַבֹּקֶר אֲשֶׁר נֶאֱמַר אֱמֶת הוּא וְאַתָּה סְתֹם הֶחָזוֹן כִּי לְיָמִים רַבִּים׃

27 So I, *Daniel*, was stricken, and languished many days. Then I arose and attended to the king's business, but I was dismayed by the vision and no one could explain it.

כז וַאֲנִי דָנִיֵּאל נִהְיֵיתִי וְנֶחֱלֵיתִי יָמִים וָאָקוּם וָאֶעֱשֶׂה אֶת־מְלֶאכֶת הַמֶּלֶךְ וָאֶשְׁתּוֹמֵם עַל־הַמַּרְאֶה וְאֵין מֵבִין׃

8:21 And the buck, the he-goat – the king of Greece In *Daniel*'s first vision, the second and third kingdoms are represented by vicious beasts – a bear and a leopard. In this vision, they are represented by more tame animals – the ram and the he-goat. Rabbi Yitzchak Abrabanel explains that the first vision depicts the empires' objective strength, while the second vision portrays how these kingdoms treated the Jewish people and the Land of Israel. The Persian-Median empire, as well as the Greeks, were extremely powerful nations who conquered the entire known world at the time. Despite their might, these nations dealt relatively kindly with the Children of Israel. During Persian-Median rule, Cyrus encouraged the Jews to return to Israel. Darius allowed the completion of the Temple's construction, and Xerxes provided material to help this cause. Alexander the Great, the first ruler of Greece, retreated peacefully from *Yerushalayim*. Only later, under the rule of Antiochus, did the Jews really begin to suffer.

A mountain goat at the Ramon Crater

9 ¹ In the first year of Darius son of Ahasuerus, of Median descent, who was made king over the kingdom of the Chaldeans –

ט א בִּשְׁנַת אַחַת לְדָרְיָ֫וֶשׁ בֶּן־אֲחַשְׁוֵר֑וֹשׁ מִזֶּ֖רַע מָדָ֑י אֲשֶׁ֣ר הָמְלַ֔ךְ עַ֖ל מַלְכ֥וּת כַּשְׂדִּֽים׃

² in the first year of his reign, I, *Daniel*, consulted the books concerning the number of years that, according to the word of *Hashem* that had come to *Yirmiyahu* the *Navi*, were to be the term of *Yerushalayim*'s desolation – seventy years.

ב בִּשְׁנַ֤ת אַחַת֙ לְמָלְכ֔וֹ אֲנִי֙ דָּנִיֵּ֔אל בִּינֹ֖תִי בַּסְּפָרִ֑ים מִסְפַּ֣ר הַשָּׁנִ֗ים אֲשֶׁ֨ר הָיָ֤ה דְבַר־יְהֹוָה֙ אֶל־יִרְמְיָ֣ה הַנָּבִ֔יא לְמַלֹּ֛אות לְחׇרְב֥וֹת יְרוּשָׁלַ֖͏ִם שִׁבְעִ֥ים שָׁנָֽה׃

³ I turned my face to *Hashem*, devoting myself to prayer and supplication, in fasting, in sackcloth and ashes.

ג וָאֶתְּנָ֣ה אֶת־פָּנַ֗י אֶל־אֲדֹנָ֤י הָאֱלֹהִים֙ לְבַקֵּ֣שׁ תְּפִלָּ֔ה וְתַחֲנוּנִ֑ים בְּצ֥וֹם וְשַׂ֖ק וָאֵֽפֶר׃

⁴ I prayed to *Hashem* my God, making confession thus: "O *Hashem*, great and awesome God, who stays faithful to His covenant with those who love Him and keep His commandments!

ד וָאֶתְפַּֽלְלָ֛ה לַיהֹוָ֥ה אֱלֹהַ֖י וָאֶתְוַדֶּ֑ה וָאֹֽמְרָ֗ה אָ֤נָּא אֲדֹנָי֙ הָאֵ֤ל הַגָּדוֹל֙ וְהַנּוֹרָ֔א שֹׁמֵ֤ר הַבְּרִית֙ וְהַחֶ֔סֶד לְאֹהֲבָ֖יו וּלְשֹֽׁמְרֵ֥י מִצְוֺתָֽיו׃

⁵ We have sinned; we have gone astray; we have acted wickedly; we have been rebellious and have deviated from Your commandments and Your rules,

ה חָטָ֥אנוּ וְעָוִ֖ינוּ [והרשענו] [הִרְשַׁ֣עְנוּ] וּמָרָ֑דְנוּ וְס֥וֹר מִמִּצְוֺתֶ֖ךָ וּמִמִּשְׁפָּטֶֽיךָ׃

⁶ and have not obeyed Your servants the *neviim* who spoke in Your name to our kings, our officers, our fathers, and all the people of the land.

ו וְלֹ֤א שָׁמַ֙עְנוּ֙ אֶל־עֲבָדֶ֣יךָ הַנְּבִיאִ֔ים אֲשֶׁ֤ר דִּבְּרוּ֙ בְּשִׁמְךָ֔ אֶל־מְלָכֵ֥ינוּ שָׂרֵ֖ינוּ וַאֲבֹתֵ֑ינוּ וְאֶ֖ל כׇּל־עַ֥ם הָאָֽרֶץ׃

⁷ With You, O *Hashem*, is the right, and the shame is on us to this very day, on the men of *Yehuda* and the inhabitants of *Yerushalayim*, all *Yisrael*, near and far, in all the lands where You have banished them, for the trespass they committed against You.

ז לְךָ֤ אֲדֹנָי֙ הַצְּדָקָ֔ה וְלָ֛נוּ בֹּ֥שֶׁת הַפָּנִ֖ים כַּיּ֣וֹם הַזֶּ֑ה לְאִ֣ישׁ יְהוּדָ֗ה וּלְיֹשְׁבֵ֣י יְרוּשָׁלַ֜͏ִם וּֽלְכׇל־יִשְׂרָאֵ֗ל הַקְּרֹבִ֤ים וְהָֽרְחֹקִים֙ בְּכׇל־הָ֣אֲרָצ֔וֹת אֲשֶׁ֥ר הִדַּחְתָּ֖ם שָׁ֑ם בְּמַעֲלָ֖ם אֲשֶׁ֥ר מָֽעֲלוּ־בָֽךְ׃

⁸ The shame, *Hashem*, is on us, on our kings, our officers, and our fathers, because we have sinned against You.

ח יְהֹוָ֗ה לָ֚נוּ בֹּ֣שֶׁת הַפָּנִ֔ים לִמְלָכֵ֥ינוּ לְשָׂרֵ֖ינוּ וְלַאֲבֹתֵ֑ינוּ אֲשֶׁ֥ר חָטָ֖אנוּ לָֽךְ׃

⁹ To *Hashem* our God belong mercy and forgiveness, for we rebelled against Him,

ט לַֽאדֹנָ֣י אֱלֹהֵ֔ינוּ הָרַחֲמִ֖ים וְהַסְּלִח֑וֹת כִּ֥י מָרַ֖דְנוּ בּֽוֹ׃

¹⁰ and did not obey *Hashem* our God by following His teachings that He set before us through His servants the *neviim*.

י וְלֹ֣א שָׁמַ֔עְנוּ בְּק֖וֹל יְהֹוָ֣ה אֱלֹהֵ֑ינוּ לָלֶ֤כֶת בְּתֽוֹרֹתָיו֙ אֲשֶׁ֣ר נָתַ֣ן לְפָנֵ֔ינוּ בְּיַ֖ד עֲבָדָ֥יו הַנְּבִיאִֽים׃

¹¹ All *Yisrael* has violated Your teaching and gone astray, disobeying You; so the curse and the oath written in the Teaching of *Moshe*, the servant of *Hashem*, have been poured down upon us, for we have sinned against Him.

יא וְכׇל־יִשְׂרָאֵ֗ל עָֽבְרוּ֙ אֶת־תּ֣וֹרָתֶ֔ךָ וְס֕וֹר לְבִלְתִּ֖י שְׁמ֣וֹעַ בְּקֹלֶ֑ךָ וַתִּתַּ֨ךְ עָלֵ֜ינוּ הָאָלָ֣ה וְהַשְּׁבֻעָ֗ה אֲשֶׁ֤ר כְּתוּבָה֙ בְּתוֹרַת֙ מֹשֶׁ֣ה עֶֽבֶד־הָֽאֱלֹהִ֔ים כִּ֥י חָטָ֖אנוּ לֽוֹ׃

12 He carried out the threat that He made against us, and against our rulers who ruled us, to bring upon us great misfortune; under the whole heaven there has never been done the like of what was done to *Yerushalayim.*

יב וַיָּ֩קֶם֩ אֶת־דְּבָרָ֨ו [דְּבָרֹ֜ו] אֲשֶׁר־דִּבֶּ֣ר עָלֵ֗ינוּ וְעַ֤ל שֹׁפְטֵ֙ינוּ֙ אֲשֶׁ֣ר שְׁפָט֔וּנוּ לְהָבִ֥יא עָלֵ֖ינוּ רָעָ֣ה גְדֹלָ֑ה אֲשֶׁ֣ר לֹֽא־נֶעֶשְׂתָ֗ה תַּ֚חַת כָּל־הַשָּׁמַ֔יִם כַּאֲשֶׁ֥ר נֶעֶשְׂתָ֖ה בִּירוּשָׁלָֽ͏ִם:

13 All that calamity, just as is written in the Teaching of *Moshe,* came upon us, yet we did not supplicate *Hashem* our God, did not repent of our iniquity or become wise through Your truth.

יג כַּאֲשֶׁ֤ר כָּתוּב֙ בְּתוֹרַ֣ת מֹשֶׁ֔ה אֵ֛ת כָּל־הָרָעָ֥ה הַזֹּ֖את בָּ֣אָה עָלֵ֑ינוּ וְלֹֽא־חִלִּ֜ינוּ אֶת־פְּנֵ֣י ׀ יְהוָ֣ה אֱלֹהֵ֗ינוּ לָשׁוּב֙ מֵֽעֲוֺנֵ֔נוּ וּלְהַשְׂכִּ֖יל בַּאֲמִתֶּֽךָ:

14 Hence *Hashem* was intent upon bringing calamity upon us, for *Hashem* our God is in the right in all that He has done, but we have not obeyed Him.

יד וַיִּשְׁקֹ֤ד יְהוָה֙ עַל־הָ֣רָעָ֔ה וַיְבִיאֶ֖הָ עָלֵ֑ינוּ כִּֽי־צַדִּ֞יק יְהוָ֣ה אֱלֹהֵ֗ינוּ עַל־כָּל־מַעֲשָׂיו֙ אֲשֶׁ֣ר עָשָׂ֔ה וְלֹ֥א שָׁמַ֖עְנוּ בְּקֹלֽוֹ:

15 "Now, *Hashem* our God – You who brought Your people out of the land of Egypt with a mighty hand, winning fame for Yourself to this very day – we have sinned, we have acted wickedly.

טו וְעַתָּ֣ה ׀ אֲדֹנָ֣י אֱלֹהֵ֗ינוּ אֲשֶׁר֩ הוֹצֵ֨אתָ אֶת־עַמְּךָ֜ מֵאֶ֤רֶץ מִצְרַ֙יִם֙ בְּיָ֣ד חֲזָקָ֔ה וַתַּֽעַשׂ־לְךָ֥ שֵׁ֖ם כַּיּ֣וֹם הַזֶּ֑ה חָטָ֖אנוּ רָשָֽׁעְנוּ:

16 O *Hashem,* as befits Your abundant benevolence, let Your wrathful fury turn back from Your city *Yerushalayim,* Your holy mountain; for because of our sins and the iniquities of our fathers, *Yerushalayim* and Your people have become a mockery among all who are around us.

טז אֲדֹנָ֗י כְּכָל־צִדְקֹתֶ֙ךָ֙ יָֽשׇׁב־נָ֤א אַפְּךָ֙ וַחֲמָ֣תְךָ֔ מֵעִֽירְךָ֥ יְרוּשָׁלַ֖͏ִם הַר־קָדְשֶׁ֑ךָ כִּ֤י בַחֲטָאֵ֙ינוּ֙ וּבַעֲוֺנ֣וֹת אֲבֹתֵ֔ינוּ יְרוּשָׁלַ֧͏ִם וְעַמְּךָ֛ לְחֶרְפָּ֖ה לְכָל־סְבִיבֹתֵֽינוּ:

a-do-NAI k'-khol tzid-ko-TE-kha ya-shov NA a-p'-KHA
va-kha-ma-t'-KHA may-ee-r'-KHA y'-ru-sha-LA-im har kod-SHE-kha
KEE va-kha-ta-AY-nu u-va-a-vo-NOT a-vo-TAY-nu y'-ru-sha-LA-im
v'-a-m'-KHA l'-kher-PAH l-khol s'-vee-vo-TAY-nu

17 "O our God, hear now the prayer of Your servant and his plea, and show Your favor to Your desolate sanctuary, for *Hashem*'s sake.

יז וְעַתָּ֣ה ׀ שְׁמַ֣ע אֱלֹהֵ֗ינוּ אֶל־תְּפִלַּ֤ת עַבְדְּךָ֙ וְאֶל־תַּ֣חֲנוּנָ֔יו וְהָאֵ֣ר פָּנֶ֔יךָ עַל־מִקְדָּשְׁךָ֖ הַשָּׁמֵ֑ם לְמַ֖עַן אֲדֹנָֽי:

9:16 *Yerushalayim* **and Your people have become a mockery** In his prayer, *Daniel* lists three compelling reasons for *Hashem* to accept his prayer and redeem the people from Babylonia: For the sake of *Yerushalayim,* of the *Beit Hamikdash* and of the Jewish people. Rabbi Yitzchak Abrabanel elaborates on these points. Regarding *Yerushalayim, Daniel* points out that it is an embarrassment to God when His beautiful city lies in ruins. He further questions how *Hashem* can ignore the Temple Mount where His presence was manifest most clearly on earth. Lastly, it is a desecration of God's name when His chosen people are despised. *Daniel* groups *Yerushalayim* and

Yerushalayim

the Jewish people together, "*Yerushalayim* and Your people have become a mockery among all who are around us," since the Jews and *Yerushalayim* are one. Without their holy city, how can they succeed in exile, and how can *Yerushalayim* flourish without her children? *Daniel*'s sentiments were echoed by Teddy Kollek, who served as mayor of *Yerushalayim* from 1967–1993: "For three thousand years, Jerusalem has been the center of Jewish hope and longing. No other city has played such a dominant role in the history, culture, religion and consciousness of a people as has Jerusalem in the life of Jewry and Judaism. Throughout centuries of exile, Jerusalem remained alive in the hearts of Jews everywhere as the focal point of Jewish history, the symbol of ancient glory, spiritual fulfillment and modern renewal. This heart and soul of the Jewish people engenders the thought that if you want one simple word to symbolize all of Jewish history, that word would be 'Jerusalem.'"

18 Incline Your ear, O my God, and hear; open Your
eyes and see our desolation and the city to which
Your name is attached. Not because of any merit of
ours do we lay our plea before You but because of
Your abundant mercies.

יח הַטֵּה אֱלֹהַי אָזְנְךָ וּשֲׁמָע פקחה [פְּקַח]
עֵינֶיךָ וּרְאֵה שֹׁמְמֹתֵינוּ וְהָעִיר אֲשֶׁר־
נִקְרָא שִׁמְךָ עָלֶיהָ כִּי ׀ לֹא עַל־צִדְקֹתֵינוּ
אֲנַחְנוּ מַפִּילִים תַּחֲנוּנֵינוּ לְפָנֶיךָ כִּי עַל־
רַחֲמֶיךָ הָרַבִּים:

19 O *Hashem*, hear! O *Hashem*, forgive! O *Hashem*,
listen, and act without delay for Your own sake, O
my God; for Your name is attached to Your city and
Your people!"

יט אֲדֹנָי ׀ שְׁמָעָה אֲדֹנָי ׀ סְלָחָה אֲדֹנָי
הַקְשִׁיבָה וַעֲשֵׂה אַל־תְּאַחַר לְמַעֲנְךָ
אֱלֹהַי כִּי־שִׁמְךָ נִקְרָא עַל־עִירְךָ וְעַל־
עַמֶּךָ:

20 While I was speaking, praying, and confessing my
sin and the sin of my people *Yisrael*, and laying my
supplication before *Hashem* my God on behalf of
the holy mountain of my God –

כ וְעוֹד אֲנִי מְדַבֵּר וּמִתְפַּלֵּל וּמִתְוַדֶּה
חַטָּאתִי וְחַטַּאת עַמִּי יִשְׂרָאֵל וּמַפִּיל
תְּחִנָּתִי לִפְנֵי יְהֹוָה אֱלֹהַי עַל הַר־קֹדֶשׁ
אֱלֹהָי:

21 while I was uttering my prayer, the man Gabriel,
whom I had previously seen in the vision, was sent
forth in flight and reached me about the time of the
evening offering.

כא וְעוֹד אֲנִי מְדַבֵּר בַּתְּפִלָּה וְהָאִישׁ
גַּבְרִיאֵל אֲשֶׁר רָאִיתִי בֶחָזוֹן בַּתְּחִלָּה
מֻעָף בִּיעָף נֹגֵעַ אֵלַי כְּעֵת מִנְחַת־עָרֶב:

22 He made me understand by speaking to me and
saying, "Daniel, I have just come forth to give you
understanding.

כב וַיָּבֶן וַיְדַבֵּר עִמִּי וַיֹּאמַר דָּנִיֵּאל עַתָּה
יָצָאתִי לְהַשְׂכִּילְךָ בִינָה:

23 A word went forth as you began your plea, and I
have come to tell it, for you are precious; so mark
the word and understand the vision.

כג בִּתְחִלַּת תַּחֲנוּנֶיךָ יָצָא דָבָר וַאֲנִי בָּאתִי
לְהַגִּיד כִּי חֲמוּדוֹת אָתָּה וּבִין בַּדָּבָר
וְהָבֵן בַּמַּרְאֶה:

24 "Seventy weeks have been decreed for your
people and your holy city until the measure of
transgression is filled and that of sin complete,
until iniquity is expiated, and eternal righteousness
ushered in; and prophetic vision ratified, and the
Holy of Holies anointed.

כד שָׁבֻעִים שִׁבְעִים נֶחְתַּךְ עַל־עַמְּךָ וְעַל־
עִיר קָדְשֶׁךָ לְכַלֵּא הַפֶּשַׁע ולחתם
[וּלְהָתֵם] חטאות [חַטָּאת] וּלְכַפֵּר
עָוֹן וּלְהָבִיא צֶדֶק עֹלָמִים וְלַחְתֹּם חָזוֹן
וְנָבִיא וְלִמְשֹׁחַ קֹדֶשׁ קָדָשִׁים:

25 You must know and understand: From the issuance
of the word to restore and rebuild *Yerushalayim*
until the [time of the] anointed leader is seven
weeks; and for sixty-two weeks it will be rebuilt,
square and moat, but in a time of distress.

כה וְתֵדַע וְתַשְׂכֵּל מִן־מֹצָא דָבָר לְהָשִׁיב
וְלִבְנוֹת יְרוּשָׁלַםִ עַד־מָשִׁיחַ נָגִיד
שָׁבֻעִים שִׁבְעָה וְשָׁבֻעִים שִׁשִּׁים וּשְׁנַיִם
תָּשׁוּב וְנִבְנְתָה רְחוֹב וְחָרוּץ וּבְצוֹק
הָעִתִּים:

26 And after those sixty-two weeks, the anointed one
will disappear and vanish. The army of a leader who
is to come will destroy the city and the sanctuary,
but its end will come through a flood. Desolation is
decreed until the end of war.

כו וְאַחֲרֵי הַשָּׁבֻעִים שִׁשִּׁים וּשְׁנַיִם יִכָּרֵת
מָשִׁיחַ וְאֵין לוֹ וְהָעִיר וְהַקֹּדֶשׁ יַשְׁחִית
עַם נָגִיד הַבָּא וְקִצּוֹ בַשֶּׁטֶף וְעַד קֵץ
מִלְחָמָה נֶחֱרֶצֶת שֹׁמֵמוֹת:

27 During one week he will make a firm covenant
with many. For half a week he will put a stop to the
sacrifice and the meal offering. At the corner [of
the *Mizbayach*] will be an appalling abomination
until the decreed destruction will be poured down
upon the appalling thing."

כז וְהִגְבִּיר בְּרִית לָרַבִּים שָׁבוּעַ אֶחָד וַחֲצִי
הַשָּׁבוּעַ יַשְׁבִּית זֶבַח וּמִנְחָה וְעַל כְּנַף
שִׁקּוּצִים מְשֹׁמֵם וְעַד־כָּלָה וְנֶחֱרָצָה
תִּתַּךְ עַל־שֹׁמֵם:

10

1 In the third year of King Cyrus of Persia, an oracle was revealed to *Daniel*, who was called Belteshazzar. That oracle was true, but it was a great task to understand the prophecy; understanding came to him through the vision.

א בִּשְׁנַת שָׁלוֹשׁ לְכוֹרֶשׁ מֶלֶךְ פָּרַס דָּבָר נִגְלָה לְדָנִיֵּאל אֲשֶׁר־נִקְרָא שְׁמוֹ בֵּלְטְשַׁאצַּר וֶאֱמֶת הַדָּבָר וְצָבָא גָדוֹל וּבִין אֶת־הַדָּבָר וּבִינָה לוֹ בַּמַּרְאֶה:

2 At that time, I, *Daniel*, kept three full weeks of mourning.

ב בַּיָּמִים הָהֵם אֲנִי דָנִיֵּאל הָיִיתִי מִתְאַבֵּל שְׁלֹשָׁה שָׁבֻעִים יָמִים:

ba-ya-MEEM ha-HAYM a-NEE da-ni-YAYL ha-YEE-tee mit-a-BAYL sh'-lo-SHAH sha-vu-EEM ya-MEEM

3 I ate no tasty food, nor did any meat or wine enter my mouth. I did not anoint myself until the three weeks were over.

ג לֶחֶם חֲמֻדוֹת לֹא אָכַלְתִּי וּבָשָׂר וָיַיִן לֹא־בָא אֶל־פִּי וְסוֹךְ לֹא־סָכְתִּי עַד־מְלֹאת שְׁלֹשֶׁת שָׁבֻעִים יָמִים:

4 It was on the twenty-fourth day of the first month, when I was on the bank of the great river – the Tigris –

ד וּבְיוֹם עֶשְׂרִים וְאַרְבָּעָה לַחֹדֶשׁ הָרִאשׁוֹן וַאֲנִי הָיִיתִי עַל יַד הַנָּהָר הַגָּדוֹל הוּא חִדָּקֶל:

5 that I looked and saw a man dressed in linen, his loins girt in fine gold.

ה וָאֶשָּׂא אֶת־עֵינַי וָאֵרֶא וְהִנֵּה אִישׁ־אֶחָד לָבוּשׁ בַּדִּים וּמָתְנָיו חֲגֻרִים בְּכֶתֶם אוּפָז:

6 His body was like beryl, his face had the appearance of lightning, his eyes were like flaming torches, his arms and legs had the color of burnished bronze, and the sound of his speech was like the noise of a multitude.

ו וּגְוִיָּתוֹ כְתַרְשִׁישׁ וּפָנָיו כְּמַרְאֵה בָרָק וְעֵינָיו כְּלַפִּידֵי אֵשׁ וּזְרֹעֹתָיו וּמַרְגְּלֹתָיו כְּעֵין נְחֹשֶׁת קָלָל וְקוֹל דְּבָרָיו כְּקוֹל הָמוֹן:

7 I, *Daniel*, alone saw the vision; the men who were with me did not see the vision, yet they were seized with a great terror and fled into hiding.

ז וְרָאִיתִי אֲנִי דָנִיֵּאל לְבַדִּי אֶת־הַמַּרְאָה וְהָאֲנָשִׁים אֲשֶׁר הָיוּ עִמִּי לֹא רָאוּ אֶת־הַמַּרְאָה אֲבָל חֲרָדָה גְדֹלָה נָפְלָה עֲלֵיהֶם וַיִּבְרְחוּ בְּהֵחָבֵא:

8 So I was left alone to see this great vision. I was drained of strength, my vigor was destroyed, and I could not summon up strength.

ח וַאֲנִי נִשְׁאַרְתִּי לְבַדִּי וָאֶרְאֶה אֶת־הַמַּרְאָה הַגְּדֹלָה הַזֹּאת וְלֹא נִשְׁאַר־בִּי כֹּחַ וְהוֹדִי נֶהְפַּךְ עָלַי לְמַשְׁחִית וְלֹא עָצַרְתִּי כֹּחַ:

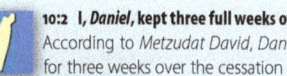

10:2 I, *Daniel*, kept three full weeks of mourning
According to *Metzudat David*, *Daniel* mourns for three weeks over the cessation of the construction of the *Beit Hamikdash* during the reign of Cyrus (Ezra 4:24). Similarly, to this day Jews mourn the destruction of *Yerushalayim* and the *Beit Hamikdash* for three weeks each year. The mourning period starts with the seventeenth of the month of *Tammuz*, the day the walls of *Yerushalayim* were breached

Mourning the destruction of the *Beit Hamikdash* on the ninth of *Av*

by the Romans in 70 CE, and culminates on the ninth of the next month, *Av*, when both the first and second Temples were set ablaze. Like *Daniel*, for part of this time Jews do not eat meat or drink wine, remembering the animal offerings and wine libations offered in the *Beit Hamikdash* that can no longer be brought. Mourning *Yerushalayim* strengthens the connection between the People of Israel and their holy city. It is said that Napoleon once passed a synagogue on the ninth of *Av* and inquired why the congregants were crying. When he was told that they were mourning their ancient Temple in Jerusalem, he is said to have responded: "Any people that can mourn an event that occurred thousands of years ago will one day return to their land."

9 I heard him speaking; and when I heard him speaking, overcome by a deep sleep, I lay prostrate on the ground.

ט וָאֶשְׁמַע אֶת־קוֹל דְּבָרָיו וּכְשָׁמְעִי אֶת־קוֹל דְּבָרָיו וַאֲנִי הָיִיתִי נִרְדָּם עַל־פָּנַי וּפָנַי אָרְצָה:

10 Then a hand touched me, and shook me onto my hands and knees.

י וְהִנֵּה־יָד נָגְעָה בִּי וַתְּנִיעֵנִי עַל־בִּרְכַּי וְכַפּוֹת יָדָי:

11 He said to me, "O *Daniel*, precious man, mark what I say to you and stand up, for I have been sent to you." After he said this to me, I stood up, trembling.

יא וַיֹּאמֶר אֵלַי דָּנִיֵּאל אִישׁ־חֲמֻדוֹת הָבֵן בַּדְּבָרִים אֲשֶׁר אָנֹכִי דֹבֵר אֵלֶיךָ וַעֲמֹד עַל־עָמְדֶךָ כִּי עַתָּה שֻׁלַּחְתִּי אֵלֶיךָ וּבְדַבְּרוֹ עִמִּי אֶת־הַדָּבָר הַזֶּה עָמַדְתִּי מַרְעִיד:

12 He then said to me, "Have no fear, *Daniel*, for from the first day that you set your mind to get understanding, practicing abstinence before your God, your prayer was heard, and I have come because of your prayer.

יב וַיֹּאמֶר אֵלַי אַל־תִּירָא דָנִיֵּאל כִּי מִן־הַיּוֹם הָרִאשׁוֹן אֲשֶׁר נָתַתָּ אֶת־לִבְּךָ לְהָבִין וּלְהִתְעַנּוֹת לִפְנֵי אֱלֹהֶיךָ נִשְׁמְעוּ דְבָרֶיךָ וַאֲנִי־בָאתִי בִּדְבָרֶיךָ:

13 However, the prince of the Persian kingdom opposed me for twenty-one days; now *Michael*, a prince of the first rank, has come to my aid, after I was detained there with the kings of Persia.

יג וְשַׂר מַלְכוּת פָּרַס עֹמֵד לְנֶגְדִּי עֶשְׂרִים וְאֶחָד יוֹם וְהִנֵּה מִיכָאֵל אַחַד הַשָּׂרִים הָרִאשֹׁנִים בָּא לְעָזְרֵנִי וַאֲנִי נוֹתַרְתִּי שָׁם אֵצֶל מַלְכֵי פָרָס:

14 So I have come to make you understand what is to befall your people in the days to come, for there is yet a vision for those days."

יד וּבָאתִי לַהֲבִינְךָ אֵת אֲשֶׁר־יִקְרָה לְעַמְּךָ בְּאַחֲרִית הַיָּמִים כִּי־עוֹד חָזוֹן לַיָּמִים:

15 While he was saying these things to me, I looked down and kept silent.

טו וּבְדַבְּרוֹ עִמִּי כַּדְּבָרִים הָאֵלֶּה נָתַתִּי פָנַי אַרְצָה וְנֶאֱלָמְתִּי:

16 Then one who looked like a man touched my lips, and I opened my mouth and spoke, saying to him who stood before me, "My lord, because of the vision, I have been seized with pangs and cannot summon strength.

טז וְהִנֵּה כִּדְמוּת בְּנֵי אָדָם נֹגֵעַ עַל־שְׂפָתָי וָאֶפְתַּח־פִּי וָאֲדַבְּרָה וָאֹמְרָה אֶל־הָעֹמֵד לְנֶגְדִּי אֲדֹנִי בַּמַּרְאָה נֶהֶפְכוּ צִירַי עָלַי וְלֹא עָצַרְתִּי כֹּחַ:

17 How can this servant of my lord speak with my lord, seeing that my strength has failed and no spirit is left in me?"

יז וְהֵיךְ יוּכַל עֶבֶד אֲדֹנִי זֶה לְדַבֵּר עִם־אֲדֹנִי זֶה וַאֲנִי מֵעַתָּה לֹא־יַעֲמָד־בִּי כֹחַ וּנְשָׁמָה לֹא נִשְׁאֲרָה־בִי:

18 He who looked like a man touched me again, and strengthened me.

יח וַיֹּסֶף וַיִּגַּע־בִּי כְּמַרְאֵה אָדָם וַיְחַזְּקֵנִי:

19 He said, "Have no fear, precious man, all will be well with you; be strong, be strong!" As he spoke with me, I was strengthened, and said, "Speak on, my lord, for you have strengthened me!"

יט וַיֹּאמֶר אַל־תִּירָא אִישׁ־חֲמֻדוֹת שָׁלוֹם לָךְ חֲזַק וַחֲזָק וּבְדַבְּרוֹ עִמִּי הִתְחַזַּקְתִּי וָאֹמְרָה יְדַבֵּר אֲדֹנִי כִּי חִזַּקְתָּנִי:

20 Then he said, "Do you know why I have come to you? Now I must go back to fight the prince of Persia. When I go off, the prince of Greece will come in.

כ וַיֹּאמֶר הֲיָדַעְתָּ לָמָּה־בָּאתִי אֵלֶיךָ וְעַתָּה אָשׁוּב לְהִלָּחֵם עִם־שַׂר פָּרָס וַאֲנִי יוֹצֵא וְהִנֵּה שַׂר־יָוָן בָּא:

21 No one is helping me against them except your prince, *Michael*. However, I will tell you what is recorded in the book of truth.*

כא אֲבָל אַגִּיד לְךָ אֶת־הָרָשׁוּם בִּכְתָב אֱמֶת וְאֵין אֶחָד מִתְחַזֵּק עִמִּי עַל־אֵלֶּה כִּי אִם־מִיכָאֵל שַׂרְכֶם:

11 ¹ "In the first year of Darius the Mede, I took my stand to strengthen and fortify him.

יא א וַאֲנִי בִּשְׁנַת אַחַת לְדָרְיָוֶשׁ הַמָּדִי עָמְדִי לְמַחֲזִיק וּלְמָעוֹז לוֹ:

² And now I will tell you the truth: Persia will have three more kings, and the fourth will be wealthier than them all; by the power he obtains through his wealth, he will stir everyone up against the kingdom of Greece.

ב וְעַתָּה אֱמֶת אַגִּיד לָךְ הִנֵּה־עוֹד שְׁלֹשָׁה מְלָכִים עֹמְדִים לְפָרַס וְהָרְבִיעִי יַעֲשִׁיר עֹשֶׁר־גָּדוֹל מִכֹּל וּכְחֶזְקָתוֹ בְעָשְׁרוֹ יָעִיר הַכֹּל אֵת מַלְכוּת יָוָן:

³ Then a warrior king will appear who will have an extensive dominion and do as he pleases.

ג וְעָמַד מֶלֶךְ גִּבּוֹר וּמָשַׁל מִמְשָׁל רַב וְעָשָׂה כִּרְצוֹנוֹ:

⁴ But after his appearance, his kingdom will be broken up and scattered to the four winds of heaven, but not for any of his posterity, nor with dominion like that which he had; for his kingdom will be uprooted and belong to others beside these.

ד וּכְעָמְדוֹ תִּשָּׁבֵר מַלְכוּתוֹ וְתֵחָץ לְאַרְבַּע רוּחוֹת הַשָּׁמָיִם וְלֹא לְאַחֲרִיתוֹ וְלֹא כְמָשְׁלוֹ אֲשֶׁר מָשָׁל כִּי תִנָּתֵשׁ מַלְכוּתוֹ וְלַאֲחֵרִים מִלְּבַד־אֵלֶּה:

⁵ "The king of the south will grow powerful; however, one of his officers will overpower him and rule, having an extensive dominion.

ה וְיֶחֱזַק מֶלֶךְ־הַנֶּגֶב וּמִן־שָׂרָיו וְיֶחֱזַק עָלָיו וּמָשָׁל מִמְשָׁל רַב מֶמְשַׁלְתּוֹ:

⁶ After some years, an alliance will be made, and the daughter of the king of the south will come to the king of the north to effect the agreement, but she will not maintain her strength, nor will his strength endure. She will be surrendered together with those who escorted her and the one who begot her and helped her during those times.

ו וּלְקֵץ שָׁנִים יִתְחַבָּרוּ וּבַת מֶלֶךְ־הַנֶּגֶב תָּבוֹא אֶל־מֶלֶךְ הַצָּפוֹן לַעֲשׂוֹת מֵישָׁרִים וְלֹא־תַעְצֹר כּוֹחַ הַזְּרוֹעַ וְלֹא יַעֲמֹד וּזְרֹעוֹ וְתִנָּתֵן הִיא וּמְבִיאֶיהָ וְהַיֹּלְדָהּ וּמַחֲזִקָהּ בָּעִתִּים:

⁷ A shoot from her stock will appear in his place, will come against the army and enter the fortress of the king of the north; he will fight and overpower them.

ז וְעָמַד מִנֵּצֶר שָׁרָשֶׁיהָ כַּנּוֹ וְיָבֹא אֶל־הַחַיִל וְיָבֹא בְּמָעוֹז מֶלֶךְ הַצָּפוֹן וְעָשָׂה בָהֶם וְהֶחֱזִיק:

⁸ He will also take their gods with their molten images and their precious vessels of silver and gold back to Egypt as booty. For some years he will leave the king of the north alone,

ח וְגַם אֱלֹהֵיהֶם עִם־נְסִכֵיהֶם עִם־כְּלֵי חֶמְדָּתָם כֶּסֶף וְזָהָב בַּשְּׁבִי יָבִא מִצְרָיִם וְהוּא שָׁנִים יַעֲמֹד מִמֶּלֶךְ הַצָּפוֹן:

⁹ who will [later] invade the realm of the king of the south, but will go back to his land.

ט וּבָא בְּמַלְכוּת מֶלֶךְ הַנֶּגֶב וְשָׁב אֶל־אַדְמָתוֹ:

¹⁰ "His sons will wage war, collecting a multitude of great armies; he will advance and sweep through as a flood, and will again wage war as far as his stronghold.

י וּבְנָו [וּבָנָיו] יִתְגָּרוּ וְאָסְפוּ הֲמוֹן חֲיָלִים רַבִּים וּבָא בוֹא וְשָׁטַף וְעָבָר וְיָשֹׁב ויתגרו [וְיִתְגָּרֶה] עַד־מעזה [מָעֻזּוֹ]:

---

* order of clauses inverted for clarity

¹¹ Then the king of the south, in a rage, will go out to do battle with him, with the king of the north. He will muster a great multitude, but the multitude will be delivered into his [foe's] power.

יא וְיִתְמַרְמַר מֶלֶךְ הַנֶּגֶב וְיָצָא וְנִלְחַם עִמּוֹ עִם־מֶלֶךְ הַצָּפוֹן וְהֶעֱמִיד הָמוֹן רָב וְנִתַּן הֶהָמוֹן בְּיָדוֹ:

¹² But when the multitude is carried off, he will grow arrogant; he will cause myriads to perish, but will not prevail.

יב וְנִשָּׂא הֶהָמוֹן ירום [וְרָם] לְבָבוֹ וְהִפִּיל רִבֹּאוֹת וְלֹא יָעוֹז:

¹³ Then the king of the north will again muster a multitude even greater than the first. After a time, a matter of years, he will advance with a great army and much baggage.

יג וְשָׁב מֶלֶךְ הַצָּפוֹן וְהֶעֱמִיד הָמוֹן רַב מִן־הָרִאשׁוֹן וּלְקֵץ הָעִתִּים שָׁנִים יָבוֹא בוֹא בְּחַיִל גָּדוֹל וּבִרְכוּשׁ רָב:

¹⁴ In those times, many will resist the king of the south, and the lawless sons of your people will assert themselves to confirm the vision, but they will fail.

יד וּבָעִתִּים הָהֵם רַבִּים יַעַמְדוּ עַל־מֶלֶךְ הַנֶּגֶב וּבְנֵי פָּרִיצֵי עַמְּךָ יִנַּשְּׂאוּ לְהַעֲמִיד חָזוֹן וְנִכְשָׁלוּ:

¹⁵ The king of the north will advance and throw up siege ramps and capture a fortress city, and the forces of the south will not hold out; even the elite of his army will be powerless to resist.

טו וְיָבֹא מֶלֶךְ הַצָּפוֹן וְיִשְׁפֹּךְ סוֹלְלָה וְלָכַד עִיר מִבְצָרוֹת וּזְרֹעוֹת הַנֶּגֶב לֹא יַעֲמֹדוּ וְעַם מִבְחָרָיו וְאֵין כֹּחַ לַעֲמֹד:

¹⁶ His opponent will do as he pleases, for none will hold out against him; he will install himself in the beautiful land with destruction within his reach.

טז וְיַעַשׂ הַבָּא אֵלָיו כִּרְצוֹנוֹ וְאֵין עוֹמֵד לְפָנָיו וְיַעֲמֹד בְּאֶרֶץ־הַצְּבִי וְכָלָה בְיָדוֹ:

¹⁷ He will set his mind upon invading the strongholds throughout his [foe's] kingdom, but in order to destroy it he will effect an agreement with him and give him a daughter in marriage; he will not succeed at it and it will not come about.

יז וְיָשֵׂם פָּנָיו לָבוֹא בְּתֹקֶף כָּל־מַלְכוּתוֹ וִישָׁרִים עִמּוֹ וְעָשָׂה וּבַת הַנָּשִׁים יִתֶּן־לוֹ לְהַשְׁחִיתָהּ וְלֹא תַעֲמֹד וְלֹא־לוֹ תִהְיֶה:

¹⁸ He will turn to the coastlands and capture many; but a consul will put an end to his insults, nay pay him back for his insults.

יח וישב [וְיָשֵׂם] פָּנָיו לְאִיִּים וְלָכַד רַבִּים וְהִשְׁבִּית קָצִין חֶרְפָּתוֹ לוֹ בִּלְתִּי חֶרְפָּתוֹ יָשִׁיב לוֹ:

¹⁹ He will head back to the strongholds of his own land, but will stumble, and fall, and vanish.

יט וְיָשֵׁב פָּנָיו לְמָעוּזֵּי אַרְצוֹ וְנִכְשַׁל וְנָפַל וְלֹא יִמָּצֵא:

²⁰ His place will be taken by one who will dispatch an officer to exact tribute for royal glory, but he will be broken in a few days, not by wrath or by war.

כ וְעָמַד עַל־כַּנּוֹ מַעֲבִיר נוֹגֵשׂ הֶדֶר מַלְכוּת וּבְיָמִים אֲחָדִים יִשָּׁבֵר וְלֹא בְאַפַּיִם וְלֹא בְמִלְחָמָה:

²¹ His place will be taken by a contemptible man, on whom royal majesty was not conferred; he will come in unawares and seize the kingdom through trickery.

כא וְעָמַד עַל־כַּנּוֹ נִבְזֶה וְלֹא־נָתְנוּ עָלָיו הוֹד מַלְכוּת וּבָא בְשַׁלְוָה וְהֶחֱזִיק מַלְכוּת בַּחֲלַקְלַקּוֹת:

²² The forces of the flood will be overwhelmed by him and will be broken, and so too the covenant leader.

כב וּזְרֹעוֹת הַשֶּׁטֶף יִשָּׁטְפוּ מִלְּפָנָיו וְיִשָּׁבֵרוּ וְגַם נְגִיד בְּרִית:

²³ And, from the time an alliance is made with him, he will practice deceit; and he will rise to power with a small band.

כג וּמִן־הִתְחַבְּר֥וּת אֵלָ֖יו יַעֲשֶׂ֣ה מִרְמָ֑ה וְעָלָ֥ה וְעָצַ֖ם בִּמְעַט־גּֽוֹי׃

²⁴ He will invade the richest of provinces unawares, and will do what his father and forefathers never did, lavishing on them spoil, booty, and wealth; he will have designs upon strongholds, but only for a time.

כד בְּשַׁלְוָ֞ה וּבְמִשְׁמַנֵּ֣י מְדִינָה֮ יָבוֹא֒ וְעָשָׂ֗ה אֲשֶׁ֨ר לֹא־עָשׂ֤וּ אֲבֹתָיו֙ וַאֲב֣וֹת אֲבֹתָ֔יו בִּזָּ֧ה וְשָׁלָ֛ל וּרְכ֖וּשׁ לָהֶ֣ם יִבְז֑וֹר וְעַ֧ל מִבְצָרִ֛ים יְחַשֵּׁ֥ב מַחְשְׁבֹתָ֖יו וְעַד־עֵֽת׃

²⁵ "He will muster his strength and courage against the king of the south with a great army. The king of the south will wage war with a very great and powerful army but will not stand fast, for they will devise plans against him.

כה וְיָעֵר֩ כֹּח֨וֹ וּלְבָב֜וֹ עַל־מֶ֣לֶךְ הַנֶּ֗גֶב בְּחַ֣יִל גָּדוֹל֒ וּמֶ֣לֶךְ הַנֶּ֗גֶב יִתְגָּרֶה֙ לַמִּלְחָמָ֔ה בְּחַֽיִל־גָּד֥וֹל וְעָצ֖וּם עַד־מְאֹ֑ד וְלֹ֣א יַעֲמֹ֔ד כִּֽי־יַחְשְׁב֥וּ עָלָ֖יו מַחֲשָׁבֽוֹת׃

²⁶ Those who eat of his food will ruin him. His army will be overwhelmed, and many will fall slain.

כו וְאֹכְלֵ֧י פַת־בָּ֛גוֹ יִשְׁבְּר֖וּהוּ וְחֵיל֣וֹ יִשְׁט֑וֹף וְנָפְל֖וּ חֲלָלִ֥ים רַבִּֽים׃

²⁷ The minds of both kings will be bent on evil; while sitting at the table together, they will lie to each other, but to no avail, for there is yet an appointed term.

כז וּשְׁנֵיהֶ֤ם הַמְּלָכִים֙ לְבָבָ֣ם לְמֵרָ֔ע וְעַל־שֻׁלְחָ֥ן אֶחָ֖ד כָּזָ֣ב יְדַבֵּ֑רוּ וְלֹ֣א תִצְלָ֔ח כִּי־ע֥וֹד קֵ֖ץ לַמּוֹעֵֽד׃

²⁸ He will return to his land with great wealth, his mind set against the holy covenant. Having done his pleasure, he will return to his land.

כח וְיָשֹׁ֤ב אַרְצוֹ֙ בִּרְכ֣וּשׁ גָּד֔וֹל וּלְבָב֖וֹ עַל־בְּרִ֣ית קֹ֑דֶשׁ וְעָשָׂ֖ה וְשָׁ֥ב לְאַרְצֽוֹ׃

²⁹ At the appointed time, he will again invade the south, but the second time will not be like the first.

כט לַמּוֹעֵ֥ד יָשׁ֖וּב וּבָ֣א בַנֶּ֑גֶב וְלֹֽא־תִהְיֶ֥ה כָרִֽאשֹׁנָ֖ה וְכָאַחֲרֹנָֽה׃

³⁰ Ships from Kittim will come against him. He will be checked, and will turn back, raging against the holy covenant. Having done his pleasure, he will then attend to those who forsake the holy covenant.

ל וּבָ֨אוּ ב֜וֹ צִיִּ֣ים כִּתִּים֮ וְנִכְאָה֒ וְשָׁ֗ב וְזָעַ֛ם עַל־בְּרִֽית־ק֖וֹדֶשׁ וְעָשָׂ֑ה וְשָׁ֣ב וְיָבֵ֔ן עַל־עֹזְבֵ֖י בְּרִ֥ית קֹֽדֶשׁ׃

³¹ Forces will be levied by him; they will desecrate the temple, the fortress; they will abolish the regular offering and set up the appalling abomination.

לא וּזְרֹעִ֖ים מִמֶּ֣נּוּ יַעֲמֹ֑דוּ וְחִלְּל֞וּ הַמִּקְדָּ֤שׁ הַמָּעוֹז֙ וְהֵסִ֣ירוּ הַתָּמִ֔יד וְנָתְנ֖וּ הַשִּׁקּ֥וּץ מְשֹׁמֵֽם׃

³² He will flatter with smooth words those who act wickedly toward the covenant, but the people devoted to their God will stand firm.

לב וּמַרְשִׁיעֵ֣י בְרִ֔ית יַחֲנִ֖יף בַּחֲלַקּ֑וֹת וְעַ֛ם יֹדְעֵ֥י אֱלֹהָ֖יו יַחֲזִ֥קוּ וְעָשֽׂוּ׃

³³ The knowledgeable among the people will make the many understand; and for a while they shall fall by sword and flame, suffer captivity and spoliation.

לג וּמַשְׂכִּ֣ילֵי עָ֔ם יָבִ֖ינוּ לָֽרַבִּ֑ים וְנִכְשְׁל֞וּ בְּחֶ֧רֶב וּבְלֶהָבָ֛ה בִּשְׁבִ֥י וּבְבִזָּ֖ה יָמִֽים׃

³⁴ In defeat, they will receive a little help, and many will join them insincerely.

לד וּבְהִכָּ֣שְׁלָ֔ם יֵעָזְר֖וּ עֵ֣זֶר מְעָ֑ט וְנִלְו֧וּ עֲלֵיהֶ֛ם רַבִּ֖ים בַּחֲלַקְלַקּֽוֹת׃

³⁵ Some of the knowledgeable will fall, that they may be refined and purged and whitened until the time of the end, for an interval still remains until the appointed time.

לה וּמִן־הַמַּשְׂכִּילִ֣ים יִכָּֽשְׁל֗וּ לִצְר֥וֹף בָּהֶ֛ם וּלְבָרֵ֥ר וְלַלְבֵּ֖ן עַד־עֵ֣ת קֵ֑ץ כִּי־ע֖וֹד לַמּוֹעֵֽד׃

36 "The king will do as he pleases; he will exalt and magnify himself above every god, and he will speak awful things against the God of gods. He will prosper until wrath is spent, and what has been decreed is accomplished.

לו וְעָשָׂה כִרְצוֹנוֹ הַמֶּלֶךְ וְיִתְרוֹמֵם וְיִתְגַּדֵּל עַל־כָּל־אֵל וְעַל אֵל אֵלִים יְדַבֵּר נִפְלָאוֹת וְהִצְלִיחַ עַד־כָּלָה זַעַם כִּי נֶחֱרָצָה נֶעֱשָׂתָה:

37 He will not have regard for the god of his ancestors or for the one dear to women; he will not have regard for any god, but will magnify himself above all.

לז וְעַל־אֱלֹהֵי אֲבֹתָיו לֹא יָבִין וְעַל־חֶמְדַּת נָשִׁים וְעַל־כָּל־אֱלוֹהַּ לֹא יָבִין כִּי עַל־כֹּל יִתְגַּדָּל:

38 He will honor the god of fortresses on his stand; he will honor with gold and silver, with precious stones and costly things, a god that his ancestors never knew.

לח וְלֶאֱלֹהַּ מָעֻזִּים עַל־כַּנּוֹ יְכַבֵּד וְלֶאֱלוֹהַּ אֲשֶׁר לֹא־יְדָעֻהוּ אֲבֹתָיו יְכַבֵּד בְּזָהָב וּבְכֶסֶף וּבְאֶבֶן יְקָרָה וּבַחֲמֻדוֹת:

39 He will deal with fortified strongholds with the help of an alien god. He will heap honor on those who acknowledge him, and will make them master over many; he will distribute land for a price.

לט וְעָשָׂה לְמִבְצְרֵי מָעֻזִּים עִם־אֱלוֹהַּ נֵכָר אֲשֶׁר הִכִּיר [יַכִּיר] יַרְבֶּה כָבוֹד וְהִמְשִׁילָם בָּרַבִּים וַאֲדָמָה יְחַלֵּק בִּמְחִיר:

40 At the time of the end, the king of the south will lock horns with him, but the king of the north will attack him with chariots and riders and many ships. He will invade lands, sweeping through them like a flood;

מ וּבְעֵת קֵץ יִתְנַגַּח עִמּוֹ מֶלֶךְ הַנֶּגֶב וְיִשְׂתָּעֵר עָלָיו מֶלֶךְ הַצָּפוֹן בְּרֶכֶב וּבְפָרָשִׁים וּבָאֳנִיּוֹת רַבּוֹת וּבָא בַאֲרָצוֹת וְשָׁטַף וְעָבָר:

41 he will invade the beautiful land, too, and many will fall, but these will escape his clutches: Edom, Moab, and the chief part of the Ammonites.

מא וּבָא בְּאֶרֶץ הַצְּבִי וְרַבּוֹת יִכָּשֵׁלוּ וְאֵלֶּה יִמָּלְטוּ מִיָּדוֹ אֱדוֹם וּמוֹאָב וְרֵאשִׁית בְּנֵי עַמּוֹן:

u-VA b'-E-retz ha-tz'-VEE v'-ra-BOT yi-ka-SHAY-lu v'-AY-leh yi-ma-l'-TU mi-ya-DO e-DOM u-mo-AV v'-ray-SHEET b'-NAY a-MON

42 He will lay his hands on lands; not even the land of Egypt will escape.

מב וְשָׁלַח יָדוֹ בַּאֲרָצוֹת וְאֶרֶץ מִצְרַיִם לֹא תִהְיֶה לִפְלֵיטָה:

43 He will gain control over treasures of gold and silver and over all the precious things of Egypt, and the Libyans and Cushites will follow at his heel.

מג וּמָשַׁל בְּמִכְמַנֵּי הַזָּהָב וְהַכֶּסֶף וּבְכֹל חֲמֻדוֹת מִצְרָיִם וְלֻבִים וְכֻשִׁים בְּמִצְעָדָיו:

44 But reports from east and north will alarm him, and he will march forth in a great fury to destroy and annihilate many.

מד וּשְׁמֻעוֹת יְבַהֲלֻהוּ מִמִּזְרָח וּמִצָּפוֹן וְיָצָא בְּחֵמָא גְדֹלָה לְהַשְׁמִיד וּלְהַחֲרִים רַבִּים:

11:41 He will invade the beautiful land Many explanations are given for the term *eretz hatzvi* (ארץ הצבי), used in this verse as a description of the Land of Israel. Our translation reads 'beautiful land,' while other commentators say that it means 'desired land.' The Talmud (*Ketubot* 112a), following the literal translation 'land of the gazelle,' draws various parallels between the gazelle and *Eretz Yisrael*. For example, just as the gazelle is swift, Israel's fruits ripen quickly. Furthermore, just as the

hide of the gazelle has the capacity to contain its body but shrinks when separated from it, so too the Land of Israel can expand to include its rightful inhabitants, but shrinks when the Jews are exiled from it. Perhaps a deeper message can be applied to Israel's inhabitants as well. In his book *Eretz Hatzvi*, Rabbi Zvi Teichman suggests that just as the land stretches to include its inhabitants, the inhabitants must also "stretch themselves" to appreciate the holiness and unique qualities of the "land of the gazelle."

ארץ הצבי

45 He will pitch his royal pavilion between the sea and the beautiful holy mountain, and he will meet his doom with no one to help him.

מה וְיִטַּע אָהֳלֵי אַפַּדְנוֹ בֵּין יַמִּים לְהַר־צְבִי־ קֹדֶשׁ וּבָא עַד־קִצּוֹ וְאֵין עוֹזֵר לוֹ:

12 1 "At that time, the great prince, *Michael,* who stands beside the sons of your people, will appear. It will be a time of trouble, the like of which has never been since the nation came into being. At that time, your people will be rescued, all who are found inscribed in the book.

יב א וּבָעֵת הַהִיא יַעֲמֹד מִיכָאֵל הַשַּׂר הַגָּדוֹל הָעֹמֵד עַל־בְּנֵי עַמֶּךָ וְהָיְתָה עֵת צָרָה אֲשֶׁר לֹא־נִהְיְתָה מִהְיוֹת גּוֹי עַד הָעֵת הַהִיא וּבָעֵת הַהִיא יִמָּלֵט עַמְּךָ כָּל־ הַנִּמְצָא כָּתוּב בַּסֵּפֶר:

2 Many of those that sleep in the dust of the earth will awake, some to eternal life, others to reproaches, to everlasting abhorrence.

ב וְרַבִּים מִיְּשֵׁנֵי אַדְמַת־עָפָר יָקִיצוּ אֵלֶּה לְחַיֵּי עוֹלָם וְאֵלֶּה לַחֲרָפוֹת לְדִרְאוֹן עוֹלָם:

3 And the knowledgeable will be radiant like the bright expanse of sky, and those who lead the many to righteousness will be like the stars forever and ever.

ג וְהַמַּשְׂכִּלִים יַזְהִרוּ כְּזֹהַר הָרָקִיעַ וּמַצְדִּיקֵי הָרַבִּים כַּכּוֹכָבִים לְעוֹלָם וָעֶד:

4 "But you, *Daniel,* keep the words secret, and seal the book until the time of the end. Many will range far and wide and knowledge will increase."

ד וְאַתָּה דָנִיֵּאל סְתֹם הַדְּבָרִים וַחֲתֹם הַסֵּפֶר עַד־עֵת קֵץ יְשֹׁטְטוּ רַבִּים וְתִרְבֶּה הַדָּעַת:

5 Then I, *Daniel,* looked and saw two others standing, one on one bank of the river, the other on the other bank of the river.

ה וְרָאִיתִי אֲנִי דָנִיֵּאל וְהִנֵּה שְׁנַיִם אֲחֵרִים עֹמְדִים אֶחָד הֵנָּה לִשְׂפַת הַיְאֹר וְאֶחָד הֵנָּה לִשְׂפַת הַיְאֹר:

6 One said to the man clothed in linen, who was above the water of the river, "How long until the end of these awful things?"

ו וַיֹּאמֶר לָאִישׁ לְבוּשׁ הַבַּדִּים אֲשֶׁר מִמַּעַל לְמֵימֵי הַיְאֹר עַד־מָתַי קֵץ הַפְּלָאוֹת:

7 Then I heard the man dressed in linen, who was above the water of the river, swear by the Ever-Living One as he lifted his right hand and his left hand to heaven: "For a time, times, and half a time; and when the breaking of the power of the holy people comes to an end, then shall all these things be fulfilled."

ז וָאֶשְׁמַע אֶת־הָאִישׁ לְבוּשׁ הַבַּדִּים אֲשֶׁר מִמַּעַל לְמֵימֵי הַיְאֹר וַיָּרֶם יְמִינוֹ וּשְׂמֹאלוֹ אֶל־הַשָּׁמַיִם וַיִּשָּׁבַע בְּחֵי הָעוֹלָם כִּי לְמוֹעֵד מוֹעֲדִים וָחֵצִי וּכְכַלּוֹת נַפֵּץ יַד־עַם־קֹדֶשׁ תִּכְלֶינָה כָל־ אֵלֶּה:

8 I heard and did not understand, so I said, "My lord, what will be the outcome of these things?"

ח וַאֲנִי שָׁמַעְתִּי וְלֹא אָבִין וָאֹמְרָה אֲדֹנִי מָה אַחֲרִית אֵלֶּה:

9 He said, "Go, *Daniel,* for these words are secret and sealed to the time of the end.

ט וַיֹּאמֶר לֵךְ דָּנִיֵּאל כִּי־סְתֻמִים וַחֲתֻמִים הַדְּבָרִים עַד־עֵת קֵץ:

va-YO-mer LAYKH da-ni-YAYL kee s'-tu-MEEM
va-kha-tu-MEEM ha-d'-va-REEM ad AYT KAYTZ

12:9 For these words are secret and sealed to the time of the end Generations of commentators have offered interpretations of the various visions in *Sefer Daniel.* Many different opinions have been suggested with regard to the specific events foretold in these prophesies. These distinct opinions do not contradict each other, however,

10 Many will be purified and purged and refined; the wicked will act wickedly and none of the wicked will understand; but the knowledgeable will understand.

י יִתְבָּרֲרוּ וְיִתְלַבְּנוּ וְיִצָּרְפוּ רַבִּים וְהִרְשִׁיעוּ רְשָׁעִים וְלֹא יָבִינוּ כָּל־רְשָׁעִים וְהַמַּשְׂכִּלִים יָבִינוּ:

11 From the time the regular offering is abolished, and an appalling abomination is set up – it will be a thousand two hundred and ninety days.

יא וּמֵעֵת הוּסַר הַתָּמִיד וְלָתֵת שִׁקּוּץ שֹׁמֵם יָמִים אֶלֶף מָאתַיִם וְתִשְׁעִים:

12 Happy the one who waits and reaches one thousand three hundred and thirty-five days.)

יב אַשְׁרֵי הַמְחַכֶּה וְיַגִּיעַ לְיָמִים אֶלֶף שְׁלֹשׁ מֵאוֹת שְׁלֹשִׁים וַחֲמִשָּׁה:

13 But you, go on to the end; you shall rest, and arise to your destiny at the end of the days."

יג וְאַתָּה לֵךְ לַקֵּץ וְתָנוּחַ וְתַעֲמֹד לְגֹרָלְךָ לְקֵץ הַיָּמִין:

because *Daniel*'s visions are deliberately vague, and hence, they can be fulfilled in numerous ways. Only in retrospect will it be possible to match up the visions with their actualization. The way in which they will ultimately be fulfilled in practice will be determined based on the Jewish people's actions, and their eagerness to return to the Land of Israel. Many possible dates for redemption have passed, but since the People of Israel were not ready, the final redemption has not yet come. At any point, however, they can improve their ways, fully embrace *Eretz Yisrael*, and return to their homeland, thus bringing about the redemption promised long ago in *Sefer Daniel*.

Greeting new immigrants to Israel at Ben Gurion airport

List of Transliterated Words in *The Israel Bible*

The following is a list of nouns which have been transliterated into Hebrew in the English translation and commentary of *The Israel Bible*:

Hebrew Name	English Name	Pronunciation	Hebrew
Achan	Achan	a-KHAN	עָכָן
Achav	Ahab	akh-AV	אַחְאָב
Achaz	Ahaz	a-KHAZ	אָחָז
Achazyahu	Ahaziah	a-khaz-YA-hu	אֲחַזְיָהוּ
Achiezer	Ahiezer	a-khee-E-zer	אֲחִיעֶזֶר
Achihud	Ahihud	a-khee-HUD	אֲחִיהוּד
Achikam	Ahikam	a-khee-KAM	אֲחִיקָם
Achilud	Ahilud	a-khee-LUD	אֲחִילוּד
Achimelech	Ahimelech	a-khee-ME-lekh	אֲחִימֶלֶךְ
Achira	Ahira	a-khee-RA	אֲחִירַע
Achisamach	Ahisamach	a-khee-sa-MAKH	אֲחִיסָמָךְ
Achitofel	Ahithophel	a-khee-TO-fel	אֲחִיתֹפֶל
Achituv	Ahitub	a-khee-TUV	אֲחִיטוּב
Achiya	Ahijah	a-khi-YAH	אֲחִיָּה
Adam	Adam	a-DAM	אָדָם
Adar	Adar	a-DAR	אֲדָר
Adoniyahu	Adonijah	a-do-ni-YA-hu	אֲדֹנִיָּהוּ
Adulam	Adullam	a-du-LAM	עֲדֻלָּם
Agur	Agur	a-GUR	אָגוּר
Aharon	Aaron	a-ha-RON	אַהֲרֹן
Amasa	Amasa	a-ma-SA	עֲמָשָׂא
Amatzya	Amaziah	a-matz-YAH	אֲמַצְיָה
Amen	Amen	a-MAYN	אָמֵן
Amiel	Ammiel	a-mee-AYL	עַמִּיאֵל
Aminadav	Amminadab	a-mee-na-DAV	עַמִּינָדָב
Amitai	Amittai	a-mi-TAI	אֲמִתַּי
Amnon	Amnon	am-NON	אַמְנֹן

Hebrew Name	English Name	Pronunciation	Hebrew
Amon	Amon	a-MON	אָמוֹן
Amos	Amos	a-MOS	עָמוֹס
Amotz	Amoz	a-MOTZ	אָמוֹץ
Amram	Amram	am-RAM	עַמְרָם
Anatot	Anathoth	a-na-TOT	עֲנָתוֹת
Aron	Ark	a-RON	אָרוֹן
Aron HaBrit	Ark of the Covenant	a-RON ha-b'-REET	אֲרוֹן הַבְּרִית
Arpachshad	Arpachshad	ar-pakh-SHAD	אַרְפַּכְשָׁד
Asa	Asa	a-SA	אָסָא
Asael	Asahel	a-sah-AYL	עֲשָׂהאֵל
Asaf	Asaph	a-SAF	אָסָף
Ashdod	Ashdod	ash-DOD	אַשְׁדּוֹד
Asher	Asher	a-SHAYR	אָשֵׁר
Ashkelon	Ashkelon	ash-k'-LON	אַשְׁקְלוֹן
Atalya	Athaliah	a-tal-YAH	עֲתַלְיָה
Avdon	Abdon	av-DON	עַבְדּוֹן
Avichayil	Abihail	a-vee-KHA-yil	אֲבִיחַיִל
Avidan	Abidan	a-vee-DAN	אֲבִידָן
Avigail	Abigail	a-vee-GA-yil	אֲבִיגַיִל
Avihu	Abihu	a-vee-HU	אֲבִיהוּא
Avimelech	Abimelech	a-vee-ME-lekh	אֲבִימֶלֶךְ
Avinadav	Abinadab	a-vee-na-DAV	אֲבִינָדָב
Aviram	Abiram	a-vee-RAM	אֲבִירָם
Avishai	Abishai	a-vee-SHAI	אֲבִישַׁי
Aviya	Abijah	a-vi-YAH	אֲבִיָּה
Aviyam	Abijam	a-vi-YAM	אֲבִיָּם
Avner	Abner	av-NAYR	אַבְנֵר
Avraham	Abraham	av-ra-HAM	אַבְרָהָם
Avram	Abram	av-RAM	אַבְרָם
Avshalom	Absalom	av-sha-LOM	אַבְשָׁלוֹם
Azarya	Azariah	a-zar-YAH	עֲזַרְיָה
Azeika	Azekah	a-zay-KAH	עֲזֵקָה
Azza	Gaza	a-ZAH	עַזָּה

Hebrew Name	English Name	Pronunciation	Hebrew
B'nei Yisrael	The Children of Israel	b'-NAY yis-ra-AYL	בְּנֵי יִשְׂרָאֵל
Barak	Barak	ba-rakh-AYL	בָּרָק
Baruch	Baruch	ba-RUKH	בָּרוּךְ
Barzilai	Barzillai	bar-zi-LAI	בַּרְזִלַּי
Basha	Baasa	ba-SHA	בַּעְשָׁא
Batsheva	Bath-sheba	bat-SHE-va	בַּת־שֶׁבַע
Be'er Sheva	Beer-sheba	b'-AYR SHE-va	בְּאֵר שֶׁבַע
Be'eri	Beeri	b'-ay-REE	בְּאֵרִי
Beit Aven	Beth-aven	bayt A-ven	בֵּית אָוֶן
Beit El	Beth-el	bayt el	בֵּית אֵל
Beit Hamikdash	Temple	bayt ha-mik-DASH	בֵּית הַמִּקְדָּשׁ
Beit Lechem	Beth-lehem	bayt LE-khem	בֵּית לֶחֶם
Beit Shean	Beth-shean	bayt sh'-AN	בֵּית שְׁאָן
Beit Shemesh	Beth-shemesh	bayt SHE-mesh	בֵּית שֶׁמֶשׁ
Berechya	Berechiah	be-rekh-YAH	בֶּרֶכְיָה
Betzalel	Bezalel	b'-tzal-AYL	בְּצַלְאֵל
Bilha	Bilhah	bil-HAH	בִּלְהָה
Binyamin	Benjamin	bin-ya-MIN	בִּנְיָמִין
Boaz	Boaz	BO-az	בֹּעַז
Buki	Bukki	bu-KEE	בֻּקִּי
Buzi	Buzi	bu-ZEE	בּוּזִי
Carmel	Carmel	kar-MEL	כַּרְמֶל
Chachalya	Hacaliah	kha-khal-YAH	חֲכַלְיָה
Chagai	Haggai	kha-GAI	חַגַּי
Chana	Hannah	kha-NAH	חַנָּה
Chanamel	Hanamel	kha-nam-AYL	חֲנַמְאֵל
Chanani	Hanani	kha-NA-nee	חֲנָנִי
Chananya	Hananiah	kha-nan-YAH	חֲנַנְיָה
Chaniel	Hanniel	kha-nee-AYL	חַנִּיאֵל
Chanoch	Enoch	kha-NOKH	חֲנוֹךְ
Chava	Eve	kha-VAH	חַוָּה
Chavakuk	Habakkuk	kha-va-KUK	חֲבַקּוּק
Chermon	Hermon	kher-MON	חֶרְמוֹן

Hebrew Name	English Name	Pronunciation	Hebrew
Chetzron	Hezron	khetz-RON	חֶצְרוֹן
Chever	Heber	KHE-ver	חֶבֶר
Chevron	Hebron	khev-RON	חֶבְרוֹן
Chilkiyahu	Hilkiah	khil-ki-YA-hu	חִלְקִיָּהוּ
Chizkiyahu	Hezekiah	khiz-ki-YA-hu	חִזְקִיָּהוּ
Chofni	Hophni	khof-NEE	חׇפְנִי
Chogla	Hoglah	khog-LAH	חׇגְלָה
Chulda	Hulda	khul-DAH	חֻלְדָּה
Chur	Hur	Khur	חוּר
Dan	Dan	Dan	דָּן
Daniel	Daniel	da-ni-YAYL	דָּנִיֵּאל
Datan	Dathan	da-TAN	דָּתָן
David	David	da-VID	דָּוִד
Devora	Deborah	d'-vo-RAH	דְּבוֹרָה
Dina	Dinah	DEE-nah	דִּינָה
Doeg Ha'adomi	Doeg the Edomite	do-AYG ha-a-do-MEE	דּוֹאֵג הָאֲדֹמִי
Efraim	Ephraim	ef-RA-yim	אֶפְרַיִם
Efrat	Ephrat	ef-RAT	אֶפְרָתָה
Efrat	Ephrathah	ef-RA-tah	אֶפְרָתָה
Ehud	Ehud	ay-HUD	אֵהוּד
Eila	Elah	AY-lah	אֵלָה
Eilon	Elon	ay-LON	אֵילוֹן
Ein Gedi	En-gedi	ayn GE-dee	עֵין גֶּדִי
Elazar	Eleazar	el-a-ZAR	אֶלְעָזָר
Elchanan	Elhanan	el-kha-NAN	אֶלְחָנָן
Eli	Eli	ay-LEE	עֵלִי
Eliav	Eliab	e-lee-AV	אֱלִיאָב
Elidad	Elidad	e-lee-DAD	אֱלִידָד
Eliezer	Eliezer	e-lee-E-zer	אֱלִיעֶזֶר
Elimelech	Elimelech	e-lee-ME-lekh	אֱלִימֶלֶךְ
Elisha	Elisha	e-lee-SHA	אֱלִישָׁע
Elishama	Elishama	e-lee-sha-MA	אֱלִישָׁמָע
Elisheva	Elisheba	e-lee-SHE-va	אֱלִישֶׁבַע

Hebrew Name	English Name	Pronunciation	Hebrew
Elitzafan	Eli-zaphan	e-lee-tza-FAN	אֱלִיצָפָן
Elitzur	Elizur	e-lee-TZUR	אֱלִיצוּר
Eliyahu	Elijah	ay-li-YA-hu	אֵלִיָּהוּ
Elkana	Elkanah	el-ka-NAH	אֶלְקָנָה
Elyasaf	Eliasaph	el-ya-SAF	אֶלְיָסָף
Elyashiv	Eliashib	el-ya-SHEEV	אֶלְיָשִׁיב
Enosh	Enosh	e-NOSH	אֱנוֹשׁ
Er	Er	ayr	עֵר
Eshtaol	Eshtaol	esh-ta-OL	אֶשְׁתָּאֹל
Esther	Esther	es-TAYR	אֶסְתֵּר
Eved Melech	Ebed-melech	E-ved ME-lekh	עֶבֶד־מֶלֶךְ
Even Ha-Ezer	Eben-Ezer	E-ven ha-E-zer	אֶבֶן הָעֵזֶר
Ever	Eber	AY-ver	עֵבֶר
Evyatar	Abiathar	ev-ya-TAR	אֶבְיָתָר
Ezra	Ezra	ez-RA	עֶזְרָא
Gad	Gad	gad	גָּד
Gadi	Gaddi	ga-DEE	גַּדִּי
Gadiel	Gaddiel	ga-dee-AYL	גַּדִּיאֵל
Gamliel	Gamaliel	gam-lee-AYL	גַּמְלִיאֵל
Gedalia	Gedaliah	g'-dal-YA (hu)	גְּדַלְיָהוּ
Gedera	Gederah	g'-day-RAH	גְּדֵרָה
Gershom	Gershom	gay-r'-SHOM	גֵּרְשׁוֹם
Gershon	Gershon	gay-r'-SHON	גֵּרְשׁוֹן
Geshem	Geshem	GE-shem	גֶּשֶׁם
Geuel	Geuel	g'-u-AYL	גְּאוּאֵל
Gidon	Gideon	gid-ON	גִּדְעוֹן
Gilad	Gilead	gil-AD	גִּלְעָד
Gilgal	Gilgal	gil-GAL	גִּלְגָּל
Giva	Gibeah	giv-AH	גִּבְעָה
Givon	Gibeon	giv-ON	גִּבְעוֹן
Hadassa	Hadassah	ha-da-SAH	הֲדַסָּה
Har Eival	Mount Ebal	ay-VAL	הַר עֵיבָל
Har Gerizim	Mount Gerizim	g'-ri-ZEEM	הַר גְּרִזִים

Hebrew Name	English Name	Pronunciation	Hebrew
Har HaBayit	Temple Mount	har ha-BA-yit	הַר הַבַּיִת
Har HaZeitim	the Mount of Olives	har ha-zay-TEEM	הַר הַזֵּיתִים
Hashem	Lord/God		
Hayman	Heman	hay-MAN	הֵימָן
Hoshea	Hosea	ho-SHAY-a	הוֹשֵׁעַ
Ido	Iddo	i-DO	עִדּוֹ
Imanu-El	Immanuel	i-MA-nu ayl	עִמָּנוּ אֵל
Ish-boshet	Ish-bosheth	eesh BO-shet	אִישׁ־בֹּשֶׁת
Itamar	Ithamar	ee-ta-MAR	אִיתָמָר
Itiel	Ithiel	ee-tee-AYL	אִיתִיאֵל
Ivtzan	Ibzan	iv-TZAN	אִבְצָן
Iyov	Job	i-YOV	אִיּוֹב
Kadmiel	Kadmiel	kad-mee-AYL	קַדְמִיאֵל
Kalev	Caleb	ka-LAYV	כָּלֵב
Keesh	Kish	keesh	קִישׁ
Kehat	Kohath	k'-HAT	קְהָת
Keinan	Kenan	kay-NAN	קֵינָן
Kemuel	Kemuel	k'-mu-AYL	קְמוּאֵל
Keruvim	Cherubim	k'-ru-VEEM	כְּרוּבִים
Kilyon	Chilion	kil-YON	כִּלְיוֹן
Kiryat Arba	Kiriath-arba	keer-YAT AR-bah	קִרְיַת אַרְבַּע
Kiryat Sefer	Kiriath-sepher	keer-YAT SAY-fer	קִרְיַת־סֵפֶר
Kiryat Ye'arim	Kiriath-jearim	keer-YAT y'-a-REEM	קִרְיַת יְעָרִים
Kislev	Chislev	kis-LAYV	כִּסְלֵו
Kohanim	Priests	ko-ha-NEEM	כֹּהֲנִים
Kohelet	Koheleth	ko-HE-let	קֹהֶלֶת
Kohen	Priest	ko-HAYN	כֹּהֵן
Kohen Gadol	High Priest	ko-HAYN ga-DOL	כֹּהֵן גָּדוֹל
Korach	Korah	KO-rakh	קֹרַח
Kushi	Cushi	ku-SHEE	כּוּשִׁי
Lachish	Lachish	la-KHEESH	לָכִישׁ
Leah	Leah	lay-AH	לֵאָה
Lemech	Lamech	LE-mekh	לֶמֶךְ

Hebrew Name	English Name	Pronunciation	Hebrew
Lemuel	Lemuel	l'-mu-AYL	לְמוֹאֵל
Levi	Levi	lay-VEE	לֵוִי
Leviim	Levites	l'-vee-IM	לְוִים
Machla	Mahlah	makh-LAH	מַחְלָה
Machlon	Mahlon	makh-LON	מַחְלוֹן
Machseya	Mahseiah	makh-say-YAH	מַחְסֵיָה
Malachi	Malachi	mal-a-KHEE	מַלְאָכִי
Manoach	Manoah	ma-NO-akh	מָנוֹחַ
Mashiach	Messiah	ma-SHEE-akh	מָשִׁיחַ
Mefiboshet	Mephibosheth	m'-fee-VO-shet	מְפִיבֹשֶׁת
Mehalalel	Mahalalel	ma-ha-lal-AYL	מַהֲלַלְאֵל
Menachem	Menahem	m'-na-KHAYM	מְנַחֵם
Menashe	Menasseh	m'-na-SHEH	מְנַשֶּׁה
Menorah	Candlestick	m'-no-RAH	מְנֹרָה
Merari	Merari	m'-ra-REE	מְרָרִי
Metushelach	Methusaleh	m'-tu-SHE-lakh	מְתוּשָׁלַח
Micha	Micah	mee-KHAH	מִיכָה
Michael	Michael	mee-kha-AYL	מִיכָאֵל
Michaihu	Micaiah	mee-KHAI-hu	מִיכָיְהוּ
Michal	Michal	mee-KHAL	מִיכַל
Milka	Milcah	mil-KAH	מִלְכָּה
Miriam	Miriam	mir-YAM	מִרְיָם
Mishael	Mishael	mee-sha-AYL	מִישָׁאֵל
Mishkan	Tabernacle	mish-KAN	מִשְׁכָּן
Mitzpa	Mizpah	mitz-PAH	מִצְפָּה
Mizbayach	Altar	miz-BAY-akh	מִזְבֵּחַ
Mordechai	Mordecai	mor-d'-KHAI	מָרְדֳכַי
Moriah	Moriah	mo-ri-YAH	מוֹרִיָּה
Moshe	Moses	mo-SHEH	מֹשֶׁה
Nachbi	Nahbi	nakh-BEE	נַחְבִּי
Nachor	Nahor	na-KHOR	נָחוֹר
Nachshon	Nahshon	nakh-SHON	נַחְשׁוֹן
Nachum	Nahum	na-KHUM	נַחוּם

Hebrew Name	English Name	Pronunciation	Hebrew
Nadav	Nadab	na-DAV	נָדָב
Naftali	Naphtali	naf-ta-LEE	נַפְתָּלִי
Naomi	Naomi	na-o-MEE	נָעֳמִי
Natan	Nathan	na-TAN	נָתָן
Naval	Nabal	na-VAL	נָבָל
Navi	Prophet	na-VEE	נָבִיא
Navot	Naboth	na-VAL	נָבָל
Nechemya	Nehemiah	n'-khem-YAH	נְחֶמְיָה
Negev	Negeb	NE-gev	נֶגֶב
Nerya	Neriah	nay-ri-YAH	נֵרִיָּה
Netanel	Nethanel	n'-tan-AYL	נְתַנְאֵל
Neviah	Prophetess	n'-vee-AH	נְבִיאָה
Neviim	Prophets	n'-vee-EEM	נְבִיאִים
Nisan	Nisan	nee-SAN	נִיסָן
Noa	Noah	no-AH	נֹעָה
Noach	Noah	NO-akh	נֹחַ
Nov	Nob	nov	נֹב
Nun	Nun	nun	נוּן
Oded	Oded	o-DAYD	עוֹדֵד
Ohola	Oholah	a-ho-LAH	אָהֳלָה
Oholiav	Oholiab	o-ha-lee-AV	אָהֳלִיאָב
Oholiva	Oholibah	a-ho-lee-VAH	אָהֳלִיבָה
Omri	Omri	om-REE	עָמְרִי
Onan	Onan	o-NAN	אוֹנָן
Otniel	Othniel	ot-nee-AYL	עָתְנִיאֵל
Ovadya	Obadiah	o-vad-YAH	עֹבַדְיָה
Oved	Obed	o-VAYD	עוֹבֵד
Oved Edom	Obed Edom	o-VAYD e-DOM	עוֹבֵד אֱדוֹם
Pagiel	Pagiel	pag-ee-AYL	פַּגְעִיאֵל
Palti	Palti	pal-TEE	פַּלְטִי
Paltiel	Paltiel	pal-tee-AYL	פַּלְטִיאֵל
Pekach	Pekah	PE-kakh	פֶּקַח
Pedael	Pedahel	p'-da-AYL	פְּדַהְאֵל

Hebrew Name	English Name	Pronunciation	Hebrew
Pekachya	Pekahiah	p'-kakh-YAH	פְּקַחְיָה
Peleg	Peleg	PE-leg	פֶּלֶג
Penina	Peninnah	p'-ni-NAH	פְּנִנָּה
Peretz	Perez	PE-retz	פֶּרֶץ
Petuel	Pethuel	p'-tu-AYL	פְּתוּאֵל
Pinchas	Phinehas	peen-KHAS	פִּינְחָס
Rachel	Rachel	ra-KHAYL	רָחֵל
Ram	Ram	ram	רָם
Rama	Ramah	ra-MAH	רָמָה
Re'u	Reu	r'-U	רְעוּ
Rechovam	Rehoboam	r'-khav-AM	רְחַבְעָם
Reuven	Reuben	r'-u-VAYN	רְאוּבֵן
Rivka	Rebecca	riv-KAH	רִבְקָה
Rut	Ruth	rut	רוּת
Salma	Salmon/Salmah	sal-MAH	שַׂלְמָה
Salmon	Salmon	sal-MON	שַׂלְמוֹן
Sara	Sarah	sa-RAH	שָׂרָה
Sarai	Sarai	sa-RAI	שָׂרַי
Selah	Selah	SE-lah	סֶלָה
Seraya	Seraiah	s'-ra-YAH	שְׂרָיָה
Serug	Serug	s'-RUG	שְׂרוּג
Setur	Sethur	s'-TUR	סְתוּר
Shaarayim	Shaaraim	sha-a-RA-yim	שַׁעֲרַיִם
Shabbat	Sabbath	sha-BAT	שַׁבַּת
Shabbatot	Sabbaths	sha-ba-TOT	שַׁבָּתוֹת
Shafan	Shaphan	sha-FAN	שָׁפָן
Shafat	Shaphat	sha-FAT	שָׁפָט
Shalem	Salem	sha-LAYM	שָׁלֵם
Shalum	Shallum	sha-LUM	שַׁלּוּם
Shamgar	Shamgar	sham-GAR	שַׁמְגַּר
Shamua	Shammua	sha-MU-a	שַׁמּוּעַ
Shaul	Saul	sha-UL	שָׁאוּל
Shealtiel	Shealtiel	sh'-al-tee-AYL	שְׁאַלְתִּיאֵל

Hebrew Name	English Name	Pronunciation	Hebrew
Shear Yashuv	Shear-Jashub	sh'-AR ya-SHUV	שְׁאָר יָשׁוּב
Shechanya	Shecaniah	sh'-khan-YAH	שְׁכַנְיָה
Shechem	Shechem	sh'-KHEM	שְׁכֶם
Sheila	Shelah	shay-LAH	שֵׁלָה
Shelach	Shelah	SHE-lakh	שֶׁלַח
Shelumiel	Shelumiel	sh'-lu-mee-AYL	שְׁלֻמִיאֵל
Shem	Shem	Shaym	שֵׁם
Shemaya	Shemaiah	sh'-ma-YAH	שְׁמַעְיָה
Sheshbatzar	Sheshbazzar	shaysh-ba-TZAR	שֵׁשְׁבַּצַּר
Shet	Seth	Shayt	שֵׁת
Shevat	Shebat	sh'-VAT	שְׁבָט
Shilo	Shiloh	shi-LOH	שִׁלֹה
Shim'i	Shimei	shim-EE	שִׁמְעִי
Shimon	Simeon	shim-ON	שִׁמְעוֹן
Shimshon	Samson	shim-SHON	שִׁמְשׁוֹן
Shlomo	Solomon	sh'-lo-MOH	שְׁלֹמֹה
Shmuel	Samuel	sh'-mu-AYL	שְׁמוּאֵל
Shofar	Horn	sho-FAR	שׁוֹפָר
Shofarot	Horns	sho-fa-ROT	שׁוֹפָרוֹת
Shomron	Samaria	sho-m'-RON	שֹׁמְרוֹן
Sivan	Sivan	see-VAN	סִיוָן
Tamar	Tamar	ta-MAR	תָּמָר
Tanakh	Hebrew Bible	ta-NAKH	תָּנַ"ךְ
Tapuach	Tappuah	ta-PU-akh	תַּפּוּחַ
Tavor	Tabor	ta-VOR	תָּבוֹר
Tekoa	Tekoa	t'-KO-a	תְּקוֹעָה
Terach	Terah	TE-rakh	תֶּרַח
Teveria	Tiberias	t'-ver-YAH	טְבֶרְיָה
Tevet	Tebeth	tay-VAYT	טֵבֵת
Tirtza	Tirzah	tir-TZAH	תִּרְצָה
Tola	Tola	to-LA	תּוֹלָע
Tzadok	Zadok	tza-DOK	צָדוֹק
Tzefanya	Zephaniah	tz'-fan-YAH	צְפַנְיָה

Hebrew Name	English Name	Pronunciation	Hebrew
Tzelofchad	Zelophehad	tz'-lo-f-KHAD	צְלָפְחָד
Tzeruya	Zeruiah	tz'-ru-YAH	צְרוּיָה
Tzfat	Safed	tz'-FAT	צְפַת
Tzidkiyahu	Zedekiah	tzid-ki-YA-hu	צִדְקִיָּהוּ
Tziklag	Ziklag	tzi-k'-LAG	צִקְלַג
Tzion	Zion	tzi-YON	צִיּוֹן
Tzipora	Zipporah	tzi-po-RAH	צִפֹּרָה
Tzora	Zorah	tzor-AH	צָרְעָה
Tzuriel	Zuriel	tzu-ree-AYL	צוּרִיאֵל
Ukal	Ucal	u-KAL	אֻכָל
Uri	Uri	u-REE	אוּרִי
Uriya	Uriah	u-ri-YAH	אוּרִיָּה
Utz	Uz	Utz	עוּץ
Uzziyahu	Uzziah	u-zi-YA-hu	עֻזִּיָּהוּ
Yaakov	Jacob	ya-a-KOV	יַעֲקֹב
Yachaziel	Jahaziel	ya-kha-zee-AYL	יַחֲזִיאֵל
Yael	Jael	ya-AYL	יָעֵל
Yaffo	Joppa/Jaffa	ya-FO	יָפוֹ
Yair	Jair	ya-EER	יָאִיר
Yakeh	Jakeh	ya-KEH	יָקֶה
Yarden	Jordan	yar-DAYN	יַרְדֵּן
Yarmut	Jarmuth	yar-MUT	יַרְמוּת
Yechezkel	Ezekiel	y'-khez-KAYL	יְחֶזְקֵאל
Yechiel	Jehiel	y'-khee-AYL	יְחִיאֵל
Yechonya	Jeconiah	y'-khon-YAH	יְכָנְיָה
Yedutun	Jeduthun	y'-du-TUN	יְדוּתוּן
Yehoachaz	Jehoahaz	y'-ho-a-KHAZ	יְהוֹאָחָז
Yehoash	Jehoash	y'-ho-ASH	יְהוֹאָש
Yehochanan	Jehohanan	y'-ho-kha-NAN	יְהוֹחָנָן
Yehonatan	Jonathan	y'-ho-na-TAN	יְהוֹנָתָן
Yehoram	Jehoram	y'-ho-RAM	יְהוֹרָם
Yehoshafat	Jehoshaphat	y'-ho-sha-FAT	יְהוֹשָׁפָט
Yehoshavat	Jehoshabeath	y'-ho-shav-AT	יְהוֹשַׁבְעַת

Hebrew Name	English Name	Pronunciation	Hebrew
Yehosheva	Jehosheba	y-ho-SHE-va	יְהוֹשֶׁבַע
Yehoshua	Joshua	y'-ho-SHU-a	יְהוֹשֻׁעַ
Yehotzadak	Jehozadak	y'-ho-tza-DAK	יְהוֹצָדָק
Yehoyachin	Jehoiachin	y'-ho-ya-KHEEN	יְהוֹיָכִין
Yehoyada	Jehoiada	y'-ho-ya-DA	יְהוֹיָדָע
Yehoyakim	Jehoiakim	y'-ho-ya-KEEM	יְהוֹיָקִים
Yehu	Jehu	yay-HU	יֵהוּא
Yehuda	Judah	y'-hu-DAH	יְהוּדָה
Yehudi	Jew	y'-hu-DEE	יְהוּדִי
Yehudim	Jews	y'-hu-DEEM	יְהוּדִים
Yered	Jared	YE-red	יֶרֶד
Yericho	Jericho	y'-ree-KHO	יְרִיחוֹ
Yerovam	Jeroboam	ya-rov-AM	יָרָבְעָם
Yerubaal	Jerubbaal	y'-ru-BA-al	יְרֻבַּעַל
Yerushalayim	Jerusalem	y'-ru-sha-LA-yim	יְרוּשָׁלַיִם
Yeshayahu	Isaiah	y'-sha-YA-hu	יְשַׁעְיָהוּ
Yeshua	Jeshua	yay-SHU-a	יֵשׁוּעַ
Yiftach	Jephthah	yif-TAKH	יִפְתָּח
Yigal	Igal	yig-AL	יִגְאָל
Yirmiyahu	Jeremiah	yir-m'-YA-hu	יִרְמְיָהוּ
Yishai	Jesse	yi-SHAI	יִשַׁי
Yisrael	Israel	yis-ra-AYL	יִשְׂרָאֵל
Yissachar	Issachar	yi-sa-KHAR	יִשָּׂשכָר
Yitzchak	Issac	yitz-KHAK	יִצְחָק
Yizrael	Jezreel	yiz-r'-EL	יִזְרְעֶאל
Yoash	Joash	yo-ASH	יוֹאָשׁ
Yoav	Joab	yo-AV	יוֹאָב
Yochanan	Johanan	yo-kha-NAN	יוֹחָנָן
Yocheved	Jochebed	yo-KHE-ved	יוֹכֶבֶד
Yoel	Joel	yo-AYL	יוֹאֵל
Yona	Jonah	yo-NAH	יוֹנָה
Yonadav	Jonadab	yo-na-DAV	יוֹנָדָב
Yonatan	Jonathan	yo-na-TAN	יוֹנָתָן

Hebrew Name	English Name	Pronunciation	Hebrew
Yoram	Joram	yo-RAM	יוֹרָם
Yosef	Joseph	yo-SAYF	יוֹסֵף
Yoshiyahu	Josiah	yo-shi-YA-hu	יֹאשִׁיָּהוּ
Yotam	Jotham	yo-TAM	יוֹתָם
Yotzadak	Jozadak	yo-tza-DAK	יוֹצָדָק
Yozavad	Jozabad	yo-za-VAD	יוֹזָבָד
Zanoach	Zanoah	za-NO-akh	זָנוֹחַ
Zecharya	Zechariah	z'-khar-YAH	זְכַרְיָה
Zerach	Zerah	ZE-rakh	זֶרַח
Zerubavel	Zerubbabel	z'-ru-ba-VEL	זְרֻבָּבֶל
Zevulun	Zebulun	z'-vu-LUN	זְבוּלֻן
Zilpa	Zilpah	zil-PAH	זִלְפָּה
Zimri	Zimri	zim-REE	זִמְרִי

Jewish Holidays

Chanukah	Hanukkah	kha-nu-KAH	חֲנֻכָּה
Pesach	Passover	PE-sakh	פֶּסַח
Purim	Purim	pu-REEM	פּוּרִים
Rosh Hashana	Jewish New Year	rosh ha-sha-NAH	רֹאשׁ הַשָּׁנָה
Shavuot	Feast of Weeks	sha-vu-OT	שָׁבוּעוֹת
Shemini Atzeret	Eight Day of Assembly	sh'-mee-NEE a-TZE-ret	שְׁמִינִי עֲצֶרֶת
Sukkot	Feast of Tabernacles	su-KOT	סֻכּוֹת
Yom Kippur	Day of Atonement	yom kee-PUR	יוֹם כִּיפוּר

Biblical Measurements

Amah	Cubit	a-MAH	אַמָּה
Amot	Cubits	a-MOT	אַמּוֹת
Bat	Bath	bat	בַּת
Batim	Baths	ba-TEEM	בָּתִּים
Beka	half-shekel	BE-ka	בֶּקַע
Chomarim	Homers	kho-ma-REEM	חֳמָרִים
Chomer	Homer	KHO-mer	חֹמֶר
Efah	Ephah	ay-FAH	אֵיפָה
Geira	Gerah	gay-RAH	גֵּרָה

Hebrew Name	English Name	Pronunciation	Hebrew
Gomed	Gomed	GO- med	גֹּמֶד
Hin	Hin	heen	הִין
Kav	kab	kav	קַב
Kesita	kesitah	k'-see-TAH	קְשִׂיטָה
Kikar	talent	ki-KAR	כִּכָּר
Kikarim	talents	ki-ka-RIM	כִּכָּרִים
Kor	kor	kor	כֹּר
Letek	lethech	LE-tek	לֶתֶךְ
Log	Log	log	לֹג
Maneh	Mina	ma-NEH	מָנֶה
Manim	Minas	ma-NEEM	מָנִים
Omer	Omer	O-mer	עֹמֶר
Pim	Pim	peem	פִּים
Se'ah	Seah	say-AH	סְאָה
Se'eem	Seahs	s'-EEM	סְאִים
Shekalim	Shekels	sh'-ka-LEEM	שְׁקָלִים
Shekel	Shekel	SHE-kel	שֶׁקֶל
Tefach	Handbreadth	TE-fakh	טֶפַח
Zeret	Span	ZE-ret	זֶרֶת

Photo Credits

Map of Modern-Day Israel and its Neighbors

The following is a map of modern-day Israel and the surrounding countries

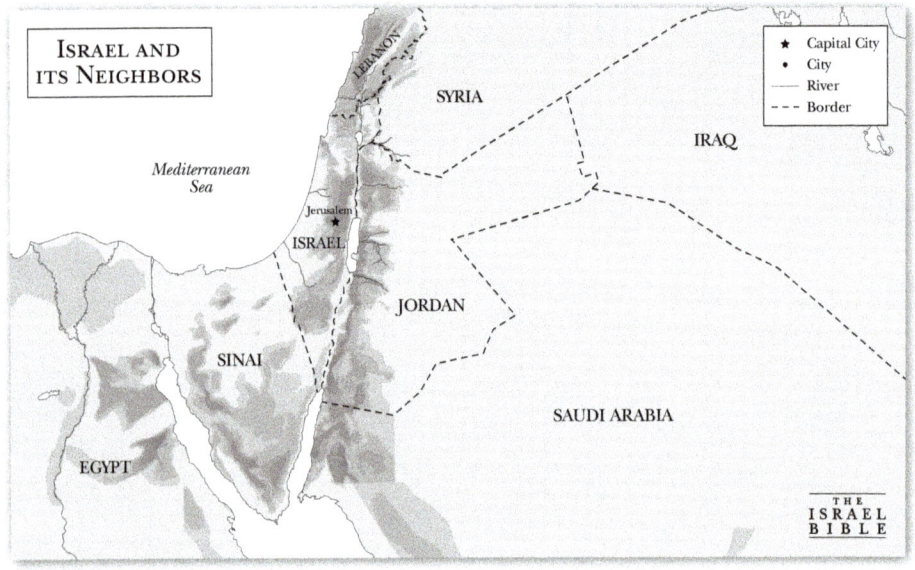

NOTES

NOTES

NOTES

NOTES

NOTES

For more inspiring commentary,
interactive maps, educational videos,
vivid photographs and more,
please visit our website

www.TheIsraelBible.com

THE
ISRAEL
BIBLE